Maryknoll Lending Library
Mrs Rosauer
4/24/65

13

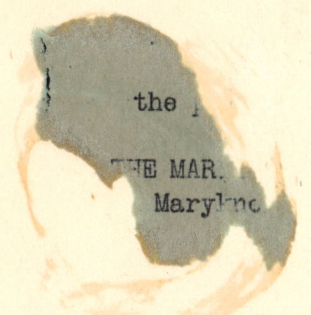

When the Sorghum Was High

When The Sorghum Was High

BY

JOHN JOSEPH CONSIDINE, M.M.

*A narrative biography of
Father Gerard A. Donovan
of Pittsburgh, Pennsylvania,
a Maryknoll Missioner slain
by bandits in Manchukuo*

BX
4705
D62C6

LONGMANS, GREEN AND CO.
NEW YORK   TORONTO

240615

Cum Permissu Superiorum

Nihil Obstat
    ARTHUR J. SCANLAN, S.T.D.
        Censor of Books

Imprimatur
    ✠ FRANCIS J. SPELLMAN, D.D.
        Archbishop of New York

Sixth Printing, August, 1943

COPYRIGHT, 1940, BY THE
CATHOLIC FOREIGN MISSION SOCIETY OF AMERICA
MARYKNOLL, NEW YORK

PRINTED IN THE UNITED STATES OF AMERICA
BY J. J. LITTLE & IVES COMPANY, NEW YORK

Preface

SOME two thousand years ago the Latin poet Horace wrote, "I shall not wholly die." He was thinking not of his soul but of his writings, which he hoped would prove immortal.

Every missioner, every apostle, whether in the homeland or in the foreign field, can also quite properly say, "I shall not wholly die," though he will not utter the sentence with Horace's meaning. For, as he gives himself to others in leading them into the household of the Faith, he bestows upon them a real part of himself. He may seem to pass away but he lives on in those who, once dead, have received life through him.

What, then, of the missioner who is called upon to meet death through violence? In a more real sense still it may be said that he does not wholly die. Saint Catherine of Siena tells us, "The blood of the martyrs is a constant fountain and invites the living to be

PREFACE

strong." The missioner who gives his life for his people has left them not only life, but courage and vigor for the pursuit of life. By permitting him this supreme act of love, God has given to such a one the privilege to confirm his people in their love.

And that is why in many a missionary heart there throbs a holy envy of Father Gerard Donovan of Maryknoll.

In the homeland, may he prompt all of us to greater courage and vigor. May he inspire many among our young to enter God's service as missioners.

✝ Francis J. Spellman
Archbishop
of New York

Contents

		PAGE
PREFACE		
CHAPTER		
I	ABOVE THE YOUGHIOGHENY	1
II	THE LOYALTY IS DECLARED	9
III	JERRY-ON-THE-JOB	16
IV	AMONG THE LORD'S ANOINTED	23
V	DELAYED SAILING	30
VI	"LORD, IT IS GOOD TO BE HERE!"	40
VII	THE NEW HORIZON	49
VIII	LIFE BEGINS ON MULEBACK	59
IX	HSING CHING WIELDS ITS CHARM	70
X	PASTOR UNDER FIRE	83
XI	KNIGHT WITHOUT ARMOR	96
XII	EYES ON A PRIZE	108
XIII	IN BORDERLANDS NO LONGER	117
XIV	DESCENT AT NIGHTFALL	124
XV	BEGINNING OF THE TRAIL	133
XVI	THE VIGIL AND ITS BREAKING	142
XVII	MISSIONER'S FAMILY	152
XVIII	TRAIL'S END	160
XIX	SALUTE	169

Reverend Gerard A. Donovan, Maryknoll missioner, born in McKeesport, Pennsylvania, October 14, 1904; slain by bandits in Manchukuo, January, 1938.

Upper left: At the Preparatory College in 1918. The future Father Bridge is second from the left; the future Father Jerry is on the extreme right. *Below*: Father Jerry in Seattle before sailing. *Center*: Father Bridge. *Upper right*: Father Geselbracht baptizing. *Lower right*: Father J. Clarence Burns after his captivity.

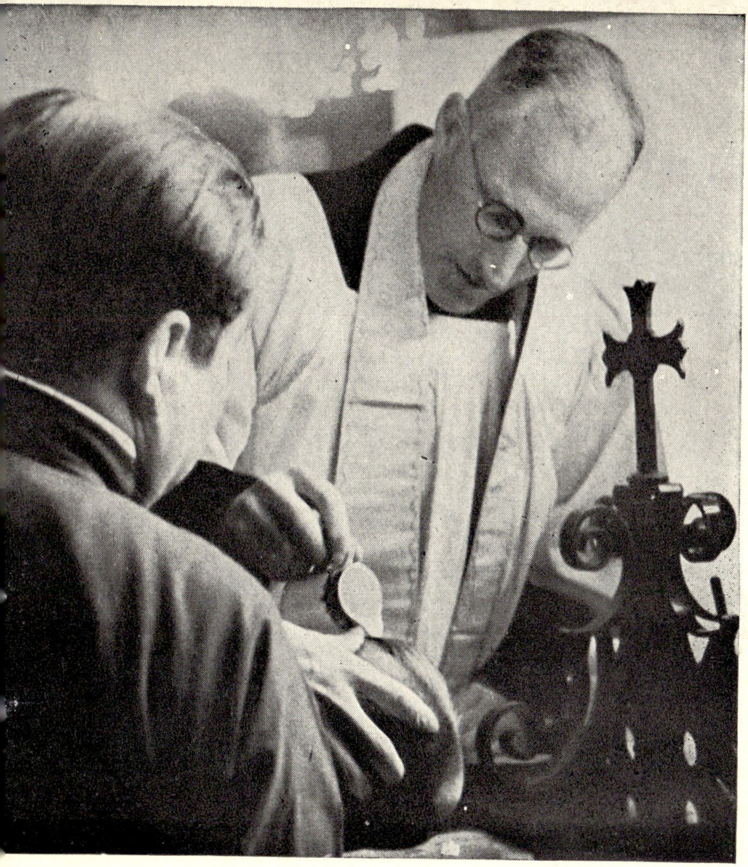

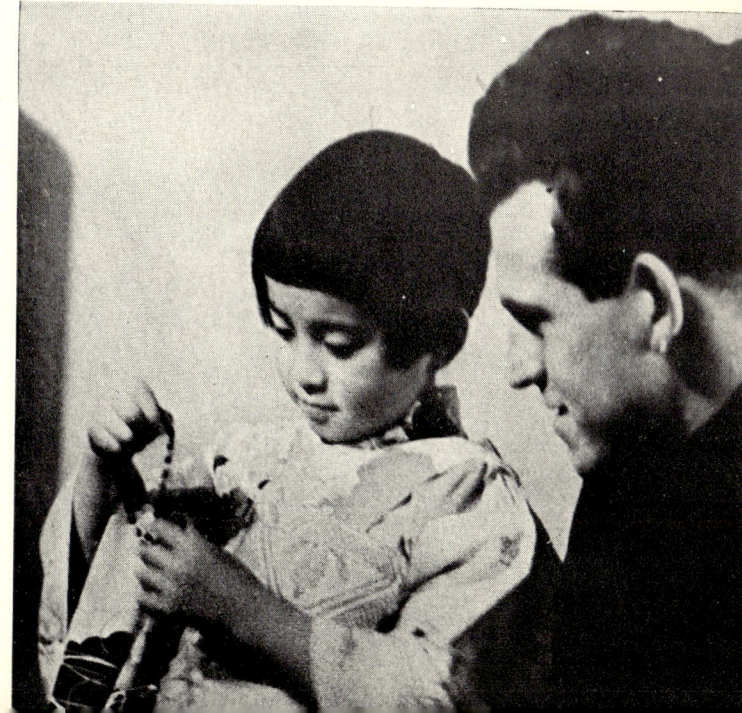

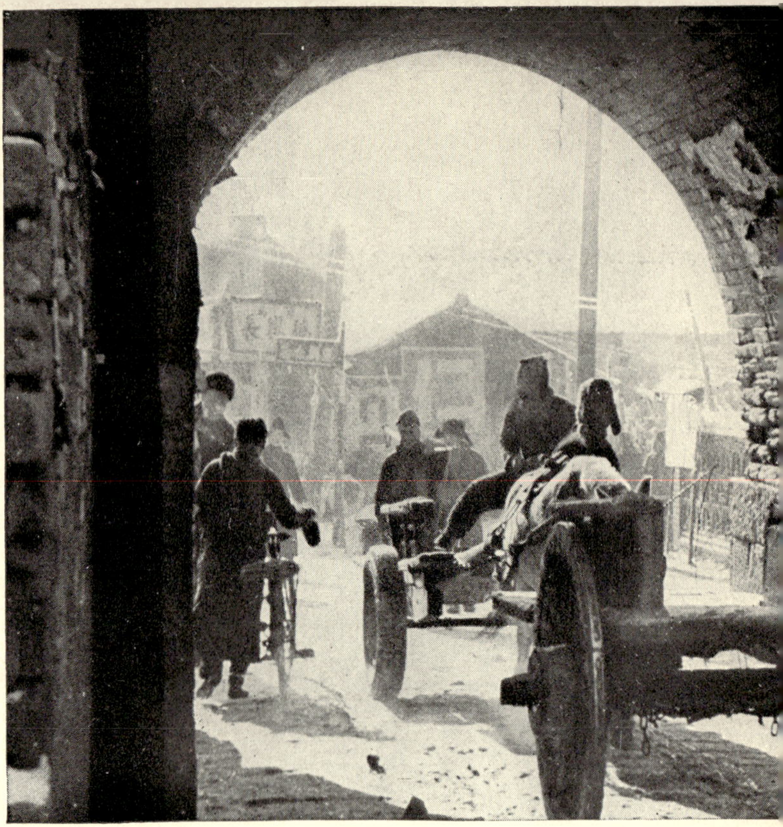

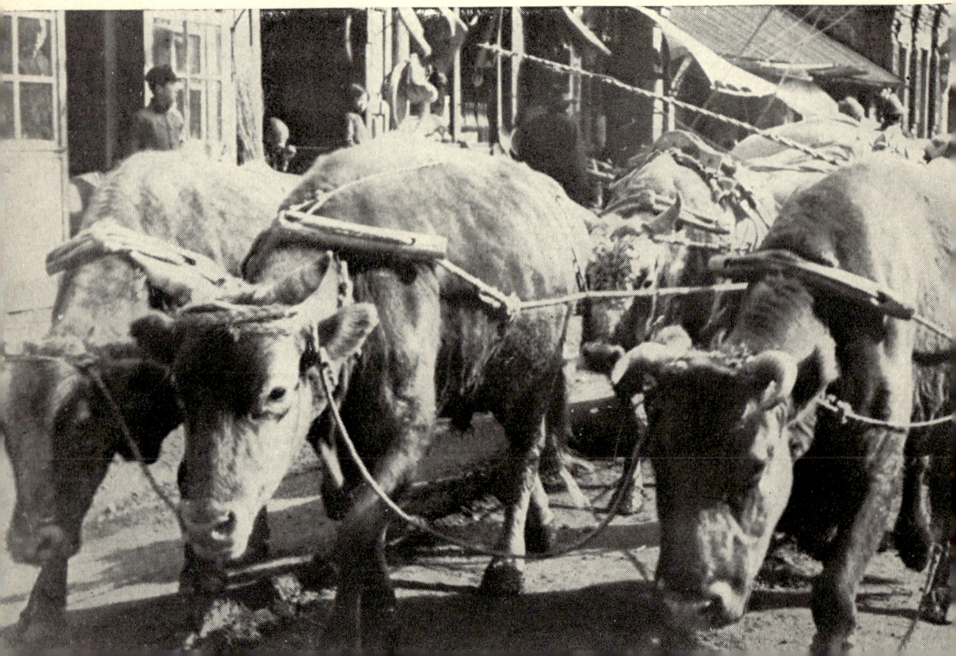

The hoary walls of Manchukuoan cities closely confine the thousands who dwell within them. Life is busy; traffic heavy. More attractive are the villages, such as Cha-Kou pictured above with the tower of its mission church visible. The combination of fertile valley and bald mountains is typical of much of the Maryknoll country in Manchukuo.

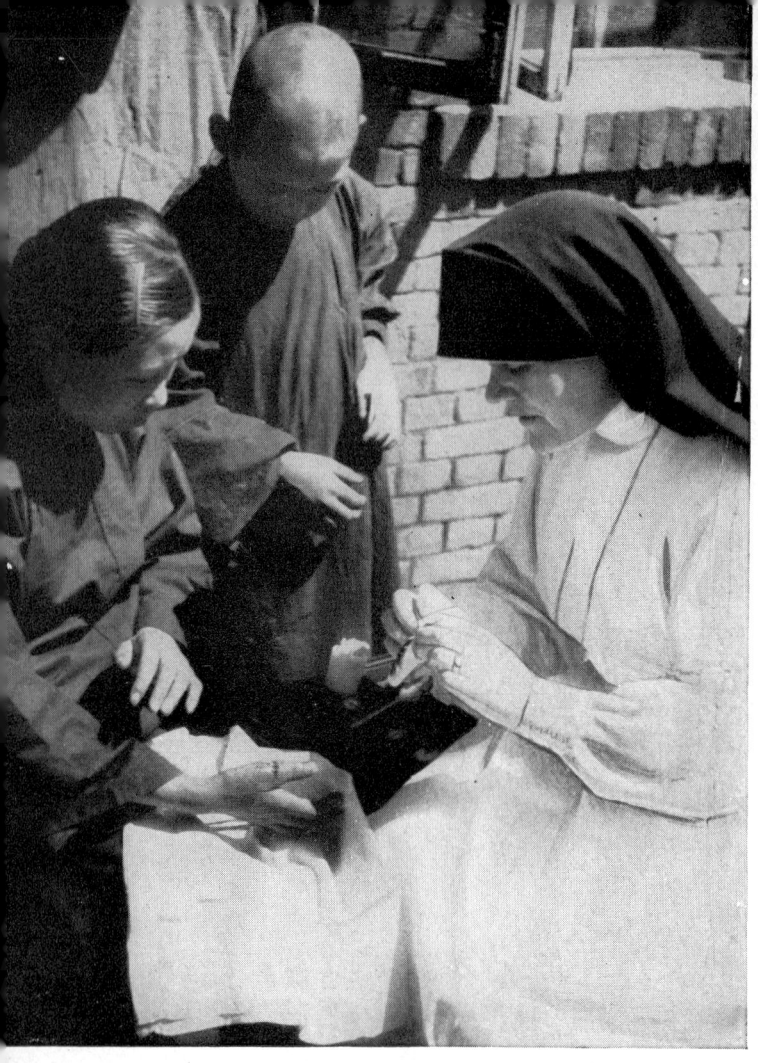

Mission life in Manchukuo, even in the disturbed years of Father Jerry's day, was active and intense. *Above:* A Maryknoll Sister caring for a patient in the dispensary. *Upper right: Corpus Christi* procession. *Center right:* Outdoor ceremony at a pioneer station. *Lower right:* The seminary choir.

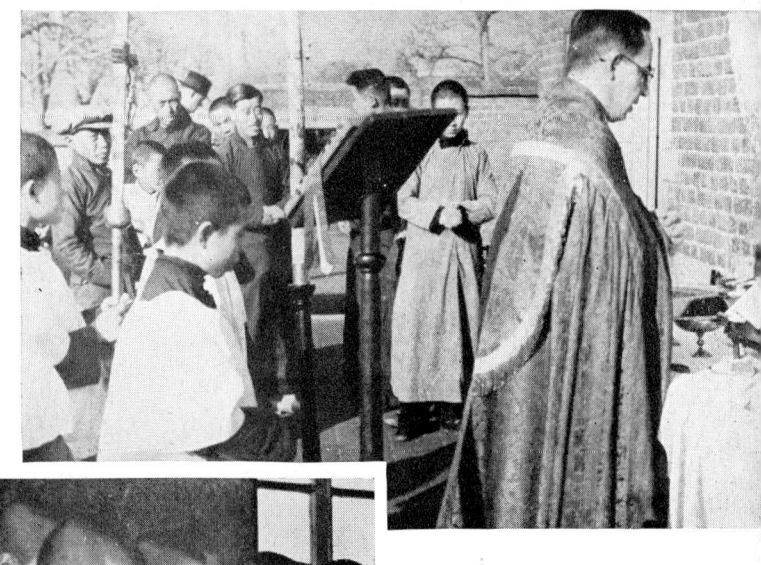

"SCHOOL'S OUT!"
The class marches decorously to the gate before being disbanded.

Father Escalante, Father Jerry's curate at Hsing Ching, shows a book of American cartoons to a delighted audience.

Father Jerry, as does every other missioner, found particular satisfaction in work among the young people. However primitive it may be, a mission school is opened at every center. The schoolyard, equipped with a few simple swings and seesaws, is the playgound of the youngsters from dawn until dark.

Father Jerry ready for the outdoors.

Chinese Sisters made Father Jerry's first winter clothes of fur, corduroy, and warm though clumsy cotton padding. He needed them, for the Manchu thermometer sinks to forty degrees below zero.

Mission mules adorned with their icicled breath.

The broken line, behind the Hopei mission compound, marks the mountain pathway which figured in the kidnaping of Father Jerry.

Last photograph of Father Jerry, taken when two Japanese Catholic ladies visited the Hopei mission the day before his capture. At extreme left is Monsignor (now Bishop) Lane; next to Father Jerry is Father John J. Walsh.

A portion of an affectionate Catholic flock gathered in solemn silence to participate in the obsequies for Father Jerry at the Hopei cemetery

A seminarian tells his beads.

The crucifix, executed by Pai the woodcarver, stands at the foot of the trail leading to the frozen hills.

Manchu morning.

When the Sorghum Was High

I

Above the Youghiogheny

IN THE autumn of 1904, business throughout America was very good. The skies of Pittsburgh and its suburb, McKeesport, were sending out the red-gray smoke that spelled prosperity.

In the machine shop of the National Tube Company, Michael Donovan, plying his trade as master mechanic, was sharing in that prosperity. He was a County Kerry man who had first settled in Boston, but who later moved to McKeesport and had lived there thirty years.

On this autumn day, October 14, he was at his bench as usual, but his mind strayed sometimes from his work. He had known, when he left home in the morning, that his wife would bear him a child that day. However, the days of anxious young fatherhood were far behind him: this would be his thirteenth infant, and he had grown philosophic with the passing years. If something went wrong—and he prayed nothing would—he would be told. Otherwise, when he left his bench at six that evening, he would know how things had gone.

"It is all in God's hands," said Michael; and he knew Mary, his wife, to be a sensible woman. She, once Mary McCahill, was an Irish lass, born in Scotland of parents who had eloped from Donegal. A frail little wisp of a woman but one with indomitable courage, Mrs. Donovan had the wiry constitution that often gives a misleading appearance of weakness. The birth of each child had always brought her great joy, and she was looking forward to this latest addition to her flock.

After her father had gone to work that morning, Margie, the oldest daughter still at home, had called the midwife, and at four in the afternoon the youngest Donovan entered the world. But the midwife shook her head when she saw him, and even Margie, who was used to new babies, looked dubious. Being a practical girl, she administered private baptism without delay.

"You have a little brother," she announced importantly to Katie and the boys when she went downstairs, "and he is as good as dead."

For a few days the child kept moaning and lamenting in a queer, unbabylike way that made Katie say dismally to Dan, "He sounds like our front-gate hinges."

But Mrs. Donovan prayed over her new bairn while she cosseted him, and worried not at all. The little flame of life flickered almost to the vanishing point; then it steadied and slowly grew strong.

When Nonie, the eldest of the family, who had entered the convent of the St. Joseph Sisters in Erie, heard of the new baby, she wrote to suggest the name "Gerard" for him—after Saint Gerard Majella, a saint very popular in the early nineteen-hundreds. So "Gerard" it was when Father Fallon supplied the baptismal ceremonies at the parish font in St. Peter's.

Gerard was about a year old when the family moved to a house on Converse Street. The new home was situated at the street's end, just where it met the cliff-like side of the Youghiogheny River valley, and it was an enchanting place for a small boy. Tube mills hugged the edges of the river, but the place was by no means the usual unpleasant factory site. Had it not been for the red-gray smoke, the mills would have been almost lost to view beneath the luxurious green that flourished on the upper banks and on the hills beyond, set with picture-book towns stretching across the valley. With this wide and refreshing horizon before him, Gerard Donovan lived his childhood and boyhood.

Though he remained small for his age, he grew sturdy, with vivacity and charm. He was a good-looking child, too; in fact, when the family first moved to Converse Street the little girls in the neighborhood used to say to each other, "Let's go over and see the nice lady and the baby with the pretty yellow hair."

When he grew to boyhood, Thomas' Drug Store at the corner of Converse and Jenny Lind streets was the rallying ground where Jerry gravitated with the rest of the gang—especially with his two chums, Ray Snyder and Jerry Monaghan. Among his older friends was Doctor Jordan, liked by all the neighborhood boys, and Mr. Thomas, owner of the drug store, whose appraising eye had early settled on young Jerry Donovan.

"Will you run an errand for me, Jerry?" the druggist often asked.

"Sure, Mr. Thomas," was always the answer, and they became fast friends.

The family still belonged to St. Peter's parish where Jerry had been baptized, and, despite sister Katie's trepidation, he was enrolled at St. Peter's School. With some alarm, Katie watched him go; she was fifteen now, and for the past three years Jerry had been her especial care. Would he be careful crossing the tracks, she wondered.

But Nonie, who was at home at the time, led him out proudly and fearlessly in his new white suit, down the hill. To Sister Cosmas, who presented herself as his teacher, Nonie said with some concern, "He'll probably be tired early—he's so little!"

"No, I won't," spoke up Jerry, and he flashed a broad smile at them. Nonie gasped at seeing what the smile disclosed: a gold tooth, which investigation showed was his own dental creation and composed of gilt foil.

Nonie need not have worried about him, for, as the morning advanced, Jerry grew ever more active. When Sister Cosmas drew for the first-graders a big, fat cat on the blackboard, Jerry leaped from his seat and, running up to it, gave a series of meows and shadow-boxed with the animal fearlessly, to the delight of the other newcomers. Even Sister Cosmas had to smile.

Jerry proved precocious in his ability to learn, and within two months Sister Valeria, the principal, developed the habit of calling him from his classroom to demonstrate to visitors his skill at reading. Sister Cosmas, though proud of her pupil, protested at this exhibiting. "He's too sweet to be spoiled," she said. But Jerry was too interested in what he was doing to take any notice of such attention.

McKeesport's parishes were truly Pentecostal congregations, each with seven or eight nationalities, and St. Peter's was no exception. "I don't want my Catholics called Irish or German or Italian," Monsignor McDermott used to say. "All these nationalities are accidental; we are all one in the Lord. I have no foreign children in my school. They are all at home here."

With such a spirit as background, the Sisters of Mercy who taught at St. Peter's strove to inculcate in their pupils the importance of the conversion of all people on earth by the Church's world-wide missions. And Jerry's class bought a Chinese baby and saved pennies and tin foil to give it food and shelter. When Sister was perplexed as to how to dispose advantageously of the foil, it was Jerry the business man who was able to report that afternoon, "Sister, there's a junk man down the alley who will buy it from us."

Toward the end of Jerry's first year at school, Sister Valeria brought a young Chinese boy to the classroom one morning. "Children, this is Yee Gim, and his uncle wants him to study with you. He can't speak English, so be kind to him and help him."

[6]

The shy young Oriental was given a seat next to the excited Jerry, who welcomed him with a sunny smile. "I'll help him, Sister," he said assuringly, and a friendship began between the small American and the older boy from the East.

Jerry's quick grasp of his studies resulted in his skipping two of the six grades that comprised the elementary school. Even at that age he had a certain integrity that rather set him apart. "I have little Jerry Donovan in my room this year," said Sister Edward of the fifth grade. "Have you noticed his marvelous smile? He is a child you can't ever pass by. And he's every inch a boy," she added proudly.

What she said was true. Jerry was one with the crowd and yet not always of the crowd. Boys who were of less fine mold than he liked him in their company, but they took it for granted he would not join them in anything seriously wrong. In the fifth grade he was a member of the Safety First Club, a group of rather wild young hooligans, and he proudly wore the club emblem, a large safety pin. One of the members brought a loaded revolver to school one day and, on the way home, fired it in a spirit of bravado. Jerry was struck in the leg by a ricocheting bullet.

"No telling who," whispered the club members to him, in mortal fear of consequences.

"No telling who," repeated Jerry, as they took him to the hospital.

"Guess it was a war bullet from Germany," he said mysteriously when the authorities questioned him. All efforts to hide the facts failed, and the culprit was expelled from St. Peter's. Safety-Firster Jerry was in dismay.

II

The Loyalty is Declared

KATIE had always been Jerry's favorite among his sisters and it was to her he turned with everything that interested him during his early years. "Katie!" he would shout as he saw her coming from work evenings, and he would race up Converse Street to throw his arms around her.

"Katie, I learned a new poem today."

"Let's hear it, Jerry."

> "Birds and bees and flowers,
> Every happy day,
> Wait to greet the sunlight,
> Thankful for its ray.
>
> "All the night they're silent,
> Sleeping safe and warm;
> God who knows and loves them
> Keeps them from all harm."

"That's great, Jerry. Who taught you that?"

"Sister Cosmas. She's wonderful, Katie."

And again—"Katie, I know another poem."

"All right, let's hear it, Jerry."

> "If all the world were apple pie,
> And all the seas were ink,
> And all the trees were bread and cheese—
> What would we have to drink?"

"Who taught you that one, Jerry—Sister Cosmas, too?"

He grinned at her. "No, Katie, one of the fellows taught me that one."

Sometimes he would stand astride the footbridge that crossed the gulley, to stop her as she came along. "This is a toll bridge, madam, and no crossing if you don't pay five cents."

That payment was not really demanded, but it was Katie who spent her money for his good times. On pay days she took him to the movies; and on certain memorable Saturdays when he was older he would take the trolley into East Pittsburgh, meet Katie when she had finished her work, and go to the city with her.

But Katie had no monopoly of Jerry. The youngest in the family, with a span of twenty-four years between himself and the eldest, he was naturally the pet of them all. Dan and Tom had an especial affection for him. Dan bought him his First Communion clothes and was always ready to help in emergencies. One afternoon he was surprised to find a breathless Jerry pop up beside the crane he was operating at the mill.

"Dan, I was down swimming and a fellow stole my shoes. I'm afraid to tell Pop. Dan, will you buy me a pair of shoes?"

"Surest thing in the world, youngster—I'd buy you anything."

"Pop" was respected by his numerous brood but also was feared with a salutary fear. It was much easier to explain the loss of a pair of shoes to Dan than to Mr. Donovan, who was a strict father and a very good one, too. It was he who personally undertook the task of teaching his children their prayers. It was he who showed a small Jerry how to make the Sign of the Cross, and who with sober sternness taught him that even in his own small life God must come first.

Jerry himself showed no signs of any ostentatious piety, but he liked things religious. He was a disappointed boy when Father Shields, the curate, told him there were already enough Donovans "on the altar" and he could not be an altar boy. "But I know all the answers," said Jerry. He got the job.

Katie went daily to Mass and Jerry got into the habit of going down on the street car with her to St. Peter's, riding usually on the back platform where he could talk and fool with the conductor. Since there was not time to go back home for breakfast before school, he found a little restaurant where he could get all he wanted for fifteen cents. The waiter there grew to know that order and the small boy who gave it: "Morning, Bud. Let's have it—the same."

When Katie brought him to be vaccinated, Doctor Jordan winked at her in solemn and silent astonishment when, as Jerry took off his shirt, they both noted the enormous crucifix suspended by a cord from his neck. Jerry seldom spoke of religious matters, but his family was not greatly surprised when Mrs. Donovan told them what the boy had in mind.

"Mom," he said to her one day, during his last year at St. Peter's, "I think I'll be a priest."

"Good, Jerry. That's very beautiful."

"And I think I'd like to go to Maryknoll with Joe, Mom."

At that intention Mrs. Donovan paused. Joe, sixteen years older than Jerry, had studied for some years at St. Vincent's Abbey in Beatty, Pennsylvania; then, after hearing an appeal for volunteers made by Father Walsh, Superior General of the Catholic Foreign Mission Society, he had transferred to Maryknoll.

"Well, Jerry," said his mother, "God is in China quite as he is here. If you go there, He will be with you."

Early in May of 1917, Jerry sat down in the house on Converse Street and wrote a letter to Maryknoll. A few weeks later Father Walsh sent him a brief note of acceptance for The Venard, the Society's Preparatory School at Clarks Summit near Scranton. "Dear Mr. Donovan," it began, and Jerry felt an intense delight at the formal words. "You have chosen the highest vocation," the note ended, "and we hope and pray that God will give you many graces, that you may persevere in your noble purpose."

The summer passed quickly, and soon it was time for farewells—at home and all through the neighborhood that had seen Jerry grow to boyhood. "Goodby, Mr. Thomas." "Goodby, Dr. Jordan." "Goodby, Ray." "Goodby, Sister."

Late on an August evening, Joe and his twelve-year-old brother walked down Jenny Lind Street to the railroad station. Then Jerry had the thrill of his first long ride in a train, in a Pullman, at that. The next morning was one of the fullest and most demanding in Joe's life, for young Jerry, making his first journey and intensely interested in every phase of it, was a human dynamo and asked questions about everything.

"Where does the food come from, Joe?" he queried, as he sat in the dining car and watched the waiters appear with laden trays.

"From the kitchen, Jerry."

"Kitchen? On a train? I'd love to see it, Joe." And he did.

They all but missed the train at Philadelphia, for Jerry had to run to the counter for an ice-cream cone. But they made it.

The New York subway jam was not to his liking. "Let's walk, Joe," he called out in distress as he was pushed and pulled and knocked breathless. But soon he was journeying up the Hudson and caught the first glimpse of his new home.

"I see it, Joe. There's Maryknoll!" he shouted excitedly as they topped the crest of Sunset Hill above Ossining.

"Little man, big smile," chuckled Father Walsh to Father Price, as they watched Jerry come up the steps with his brother.

"What a slip of a youngster you are!" said Father Walsh to him. "I think we'll have to give you an examination," he added with mock seriousness.

But it sounded really serious to Jerry. The follow-

THE LOYALTY IS DECLARED

ing morning at nine o'clock there was a knock at Father Walsh's door, and in stepped the "slip of a youngster." Hands behind his back, unabashed but very much in earnest, he said: "Father Walsh, you said you wanted to give me an examination. I'm ready for it now."

Three days later the "midget Maryknoller" set out for The Venard.

III

Jerry-on-the-Job

AN OLDER student at The Venard had received a telegram from Maryknoll: "John meet my brother gray suit Scranton station two-ten. Joseph Donovan." John was there on time, and, when he saw a passenger who answered the description descending from the New York train, he hurried forward. "Are you George Donovan?" he asked.

"Nope."

So John turned to hunt further.

"But I'm Gerard Donovan," the voice called after him. Jerry and his jokes had arrived.

On the way to the Maryknoll Preparatory College, John explained things to Jerry in answer to the usual series of eager questions. There were some thirty-five students at the farm in Clarks Summit; and the property itself, about eight miles out of Scranton, had been purchased only a year earlier and was still in a primitive state of development.

But then, all Maryknoll was primitive in 1917. Father Walsh and Father Price had had their momentous little meeting in Montreal only seven years before. Six years before, both of them, encouraged by the American Hierarchy, had gone to Rome. They were received by Pope Pius X, who gave them permission to found a society by which young men would be trained and sent overseas to preach the Gospel. The date, John explained, was June 29, thereafter observed as Maryknoll Foundation Day.

In 1912 the first major-seminary students had been received at the farm on Sunset Hill in Ossining, a town some thirty miles from New York City. The property was given the name of Maryknoll, which still remains the best-known title of the Catholic Foreign Mission Society of America. The following year, four years before the arrival of Jerry, a house had been rented on Clay Avenue in Scranton, and the first group of preparatory students lived there while they attended St. Thomas College, conducted by the Christian Brothers.

In 1916 a farm in the Abington Hills was purchased, and an addition was built to the original old homestead. Then Maryknoll could boast of one farmhouse in New York State as its major seminary and a second farmhouse in Pennsylvania as its preparatory college. So far, only four priests had been ordained and no missioners yet sent overseas.

Jerry discovered from John that it was Father Walsh's admiration for a young French missionary martyr that accounted for the name given the college, "The Venard." Theophane Venard was a happy-hearted youngster born in the countryside of France, who became a missioner in Indo-China and who, after eight years of labor in the mission field, was beheaded for the Faith, in 1861, at the age of thirty-one. Father Walsh had written the young martyr's story and called the book *A Modern Martyr*.

"Father Walsh says Blessed Theophane is a fine ideal for us Americans," continued John. "As missioners we are to be cheerful and generous to the point of casualness in our generosity, not measuring the sacrifice, not even considering that we are making one. Theophane Venard was like that."

In the makeshift school building of those days, there was an upper dormitory in the attic of the original house and a lower dormitory in the annex. In this lower dormitory, with thirteen other boys, Jerry was assigned his bed. In the cramped little chapel some two feet of kneeling bench was his to use, and he had his place at the table in the dining room. It took a very short time for him to fall in line everywhere; in fact, he had the air of belonging from the very day of his arrival.

Among the nine boys in the first-year high-school class, twelve-year-old Jerry was by far the youngest. He soon became the object of many pranks on the part of the others. "Dan and the rest at home," he wrote to his mother, "used to be rough with me, but that was nothing compared to what I get here."

In his class work it was soon evident that he was outstanding. His alert, agile mind, his power of intense concentration, his retentive memory, made him one of the best students in the school. But he found plenty of time for recreation and never felt a worry about his books once he was away from them.

During that first year he reveled in the freedom of the country, in romping through the fields, in helping with the harvests; in lending a hand about the pigsty, the chicken coops, the big barn with its horses and cattle; in burrowing deep into the seemingly endless woodland. To the various sports he brought no outstanding talent, but he was an eager participant in every game—baseball, soccer, hockey, basketball. And, when an epidemic of boxing struck the school, he never knew when he had had enough.

Out in the pasture hobbled a superannuated old horse on whose back anyone could mount without a qualm. "Just what I want!" cried Jerry. "If I'm to be a missioner, I've got to know how to ride a horse."

That idea had come to him while he was still at home, when, a week before he left, he had gone with Katie to Kennywood Park to ride the ponies. To his disgust he discovered that Kennywood had only placid little animals that were led about by halters. Now he and a group of fellow enthusiasts spent many hours on old Gunpowder; a mild steed, it was true, but much better than the Kennywood ponies.

Every Venarder had a certain amount of manual labor to do and Jerry got his share of the assignments, though his smallness sometimes made people wonder if he were capable of the tasks set him. Once when he and his smile appeared at the convent door, Sister Portress' eyes twinkled as she let him in. "My, Jerry, you're not much larger than your pot of paint," she said.

It was through manual labor that he became the close friend of a student much older than himself, Francis Bridge, a World War veteran from Midland, Pennsylvania. Frank was a skillful electrician and mechanic and soon discovered that Jerry had inherited a similar aptitude. So he made him his helper and they were a striking pair together, Frank so tall and large-framed, Jerry so slight. By Jerry's last year at

The Venard, he had become very useful and was dubbed by everyone "Jerry-on-the-job."

A school paper—*Classicum*—was founded and Jerry became a regular contributor. He had an easy, attractive style, developed in part from his extensive reading which also made him an informed and interesting conversationalist. During his vacation one summer, his brother Joe remarked on his ability to explain things.

"Where do you get all your information, Jerry?"

Jerry grinned at him. "Well, you see, Mr. Carnegie builds the libraries and I read his books."

Jerry and his fellow Venarders were delighted beyond words when, early in September of 1918, their Rector, Father James E. Walsh, was chosen as a member of the first Maryknoll mission band. The group, led by Father Price, came to visit Scranton on its way to China. Father Meyer and Father Ford were the other two members.

Jerry's brother Joe was ordained in 1920 and went overseas with the third mission band, so now he had a correspondent across the Pacific. He saved the money that Katie and others sent him and mailed an offering to Joe from time to time with the proud note attached: "From one missioner to another." Another joy was his that year: his brother Tom, seven years older than he, entered The Venard. Thus there were three brothers Donovan who were Maryknollers.

Tom was behind Jerry in class, for he had worked for some years and was rusty in his studies. Jerry helped most generously. In fact, Frank Bridge and others used to say they didn't know what they would have done without the help the "little midget" gave them with their books.

In August, 1921, six Venarders, Jerry among them, set out with one of the priests for a three weeks' hike through the Poconos, dragging with them a queerly rigged cart on which they hauled their camping outfit.

During the first two days the cart broke down no less than five times, and some of them were all for abandoning the expedition. But not Jerry. For him the misfortunes proved merely occasions for laughter and witticisms. The camp cook, making apple sauce over the fire, asked Jerry for the sugar. Innocently enough he accepted the salt from the impish youngster and poured it over the apples before the hungry and horrified onlookers could intervene.

Jerry completed his studies at The Venard in 1922. "It was a hard tug to leave the dear place," he wrote to his brother Joe in the Far East, "for I love every stick and stone in it. These have been happy years."

IV

Among the Lord's Anointed

"HOW are things this evening, Ed?"

"Racing along merrily, thanks. Today I had a little case of earache which might have made trouble if Jerry Donovan hadn't attacked the sore ear with a syringe and the good ear with his jokes."

Jerry was in the major Seminary now and taking his turn as infirmarian. All care regarded as essential was bestowed on the students by the Maryknoll faculty but there was no "fondling." The student infirmarian handled the minor maladies, and the amount of attention the men received depended on how ready this student was with his time and skill.

Jerry was ready, when his turn came, with time, skill, and good humor for whatever task befell him. Besides being infirmarian, he was, at different times, house electrician in a community where hired men were rarities, and later a tree surgeon, to nurse the Maryknoll orchards and shade trees. Jerry with a medicine bottle, a sick tray, or a monkey wrench, an inevitable Donovan pun and the Donovan smile, was an institution.

His philosophy years completed in 1924, Jerry looked forward with gusto to theology. "You know, Al," he explained to a friend, "I have a theory that the best thing in the world for four smashing good years of theology is rollicking good health. Let's use these August days to put ourselves thoroughly in the pink. How about it?"

"I'm ready, Jerry."

Morning found the two starting on a swimming expedition to Croton Point, and at that pleasant spot on the Hudson the hours were whiled away between beach and river until the first shadows of late afternoon came.

"You're very light-skinned, aren't you, Jerry?" remarked Al.

"You are rather that way yourself, aren't you, Al?"

"I wonder—?"

"H'mm, so do I," said Jerry thoughtfully.

Later, on the road home, Al asked, "Do you feel especially warm, Jerry?"

"Very much so. Almost as warm as you look, Al."

Next day the horrifying truth was evident: both had severe sunburns.

"Did you notice whose feast it was yesterday, Jerry? It was that of the humorous saint, Saint Lawrence. When he was on the gridiron, he told the guards that since he was sufficiently roasted on one side they might turn him over on the other."

"H'mm, Al, we did the turning ourselves, didn't we?"

Years afterward in the mission field, Jerry and Al exchanged greetings each year on the feast of Saint Lawrence.

In Maryknoll's young days every seminarian shared with the Founder-General, Father James Anthony Walsh, every hope and anxiety of the newly established Society, and when in 1925 Father Walsh set out for a visitation of the Society's infant missions and was required to go to Rome before proceeding to the Far East, Jerry followed his Superior to the Eternal City with a letter.

Dear Father Superior,
Greetings to Maryknoll in Rome from Maryknoll at home. On Christmas night I think the words of our Departure Hymn have special force—"Let prayer be unto us a bond of tenderest love." We here at the Center will circle the whole globe with our prayers for Maryknollers, and we know that every heart will be turning back to Mary's Knoll and recalling the joys of Christmas here.

In all the great circle, though, there will be no spot more in our minds this year than Rome, for there in the heart of Christendom is the Father of Maryknoll. That you may enjoy to the full the blessings of your Christmas in Rome is the prayer of all your children in Christ.

There is a tradition at Maryknoll, as at many seminaries, of holding a classical disputation on the feast of Saint Thomas Aquinas, March 7. On that day an outstanding student sets forth in Latin, before the assembled faculty and student body, a proposition in theology and defends it against all objectors. In 1927 Jerry was announced as the Saint Thomas Day defendant, with the thesis: "Whether it was necessary for the Word of God to become incarnate in order to offer condign reparation for the human race."

Jerry liked the subject because of its particular missionary interest, and he threw himself zealously into its preparation. The result was excellent, and the participants were warmly congratulated by all. But Jerry was a severe critic of his own performance, as was evident from the note of adverse comment, in his own handwriting, which was later found attached to the thesis in the Seminary files. It listed four points in which he felt he had failed:

1) My voice was too monotonous to bring out the proper shadings in the distinctions.

2) It was not memorized but read, and so lacked life and vigor. The whole thing was too cut and dried.
3) My Latin was too English.
4) Some of my explanations were too brief to be clear.

Father Winslow, Rector of the major Seminary during Jerry's years there, often spoke highly of this student of his. "One of our best," he said. "His recitations and examination papers are characterized by their orderliness of arrangement and by the conciseness and clarity and accuracy of the matter. He has the esteem of his teachers. I have heard them give expression to their appreciation of his general excellence not only in things scholastic, but in other matters also."

And Father Tibesar, who was Jerry's spiritual director, used to say that many were deceived by Jerry's seeming casualness, his smile, and his nonsense. "Behind that smile," he said, "is a very serious, interior, spiritual and intellectual life. An outstanding characteristic is his determination to become saintly by living the spirit of the martyrs. I have watched how Theophane Venard is a reality to him and how he tries to imitate him."

The summer of 1927 found Jerry back at his old stamping grounds in the Abington Hills, this time as a counselor at Camp Venard. Tents lined the open hillside above the swimming pool, and there was a delightful outdoor life there with boys from various eastern States.

One night he became deathly ill, to the deep dismay of the boys, whose hero he had become. For all their fears he had only deep disdain. "It's just a part of the day's work, buddy," he told one of his sympathizers, between groans. After he was taken to the hospital an operation revealed a ruptured appendix. It was serious indeed, but was successfully cared for by the ever-devoted Sisters of Mercy Hospital in Scranton.

While he was still in the hospital, word came of his assignment to the Catholic University in Washington. The year before his ordination was to be devoted to special studies.

With a Maryknoll priest and three seminarian companions, Jerry arrived at the Nation's capital and took his residence near the University, in a modest little house then used by Maryknoll as its quarters.

"Quite a rookery, isn't it?" remarked Jerry as his eye caught weak spots in the establishment. He and his companions set themselves to work fixing up what they could. The high point of their mechanical work came during the Christmas holidays when Jerry and another student overhauled the entire plumbing system. In the spring, when the well got out of order, it was Jerry-on-the-job who had himself lowered to the bottom of the cistern on a "bo'sun's chair" where he made the necessary repairs.

June came, and on a smiling Sunday morning Maryknoll's "Uncle John," Bishop Dunn, Auxiliary of New York, ordained the class of 1928 to the priesthood. Katie was there to see it all, and she was the first to receive Father Jerry's blessing.

"It seems unbelievable, doesn't it, Katie?" he said breathlessly. "It's like something you see in a dream."

That afternoon Maryknoll's Superior General called the class to his room in turn and gave each member his assignment. Students and visitors gathered at the foot of the stairs and quickly ascertained by the expression on each young priest's face whether he was assigned overseas or to the homeland.

Father Gerard Donovan came down, his face wreathed in smiles, and the little crowd cheered. "Right you are!" he called to them. "It's Wuchow."

The die was cast and Father Jerry made ready to pass his mission years in the Province of Kwangsi, in South China.

V

Delayed Sailing

IT ALL happened in Brooklyn. Almost on the eve of his departure for the longed-for mission life overseas, with his sailing date only a month distant, the plan which would have sent Father Jerry to Kwangsi in 1928 was so altered that three years were to elapse before his actual departure.

Like other members of his mission band, Father Jerry during the few weeks before his going sought to make known the work of Maryknoll wherever an opportunity presented itself. When Father Kehoe, pastor of St. Thomas Aquinas Church, invited him to speak at the nine parish Masses on the Sunday of August 19, he was delighted with the chance.

He was preparing for the first Mass at half-past six when he felt sudden severe pains in his abdomen. He was more annoyed than alarmed. "What a handicap," he said to himself, "with nine Masses ahead! What will the pastor think if I do a poor job because of a tummy-ache? And what will the congregation think of this supposedly brave young missioner?"

He forced himself to the sacristy, then to the altar, and later to the pulpit for the morning's first sermon. He gave Communion to hundreds. But when, back in the sacristy, he unvested and went to the rectory, the pain had become so torturingly great that Father Jerry realized something was very wrong with him.

The housekeeper came in at that moment. "And what will you take for breakfast, Father?" she asked.

He looked at her with a wan smile. "I'll take a doctor and a priest," he said, and fell to the floor in a dead faint.

The alarmed woman called Father Kehoe, who took one look at Father Jerry and called in turn for the curate, Father Hughes, and for a doctor and an ambulance. In the ambulance with the sufferer, Father Hughes gave Father Jerry the last rites; and later he came back to the rectory with the sad news that the young missioner had acute peritonitis.

Father Jerry was a stranger to the pastor of St. Thomas Aquinas' but the older priest's deep kindliness did not let him rest with merely sending the young man to a hospital. Frantically he searched through the metropolitan area for the physician who he knew would bring the very best surgical skill to the performing of the difficult operation that was indicated.

"Doctor X—let me have Doctor X, please," he called on the telephone.

"I'm very sorry," came the answer, "but Doctor X is at this very moment at the Grand Central Station, taking a train for Chicago."

Father Kehoe put the receiver down and took it up again quickly. "Grand Central Station, please. I want you to page the entire station for Doctor X; he is due to entrain for Chicago. Please do everything possible to find him. It is very urgent."

In a short time the doctor was found and hurried to the telephone.

"Doctor, I need your advice," said Father Kehoe. "A young priest here has just been taken to the hospital, suffering with acute peritonitis. They tell me his condition is very grave. Who can take care of him?"

There was but a moment's pause, and then the doctor spoke with decision: "A hint from you is a command, Father. I am canceling my departure for Chicago and am coming immediately." The great surgeon raced to the King's County Hospital and caught the rapidly forming pus a half hour before it would have proved fatal.

Father Jerry's companions of the mission band called to see him at the hospital, and found the gay smile in evidence though a trifle wan. "Now, Father George and Father Maurice, I want no smart remarks from you. I'll catch up with you before long, and don't you think I won't."

He kept on smiling until they were gone. No one knew, though all could guess, how much it hurt him to be left behind.

Long care was needed for his recuperation, so Father Jerry was assigned to Maryknoll's Venard College in Clarks Summit, his old alma mater. There, during the next year, he was given what he disgustedly described as "sissy work"—a few Latin classes and some mathematics. He proved to be an excellent teacher, for he discovered in himself the gift of capturing his students' attention. He had a natural ability to convey knowledge clearly and to sustain interest. "Pat and Mike" jokes appeared early in his Latin classes, and there were other odd devices for opening each hour with a laugh. He taught his boys little tricks that were memory helps and encouraged them all to "act alive" and ask questions. That brought many interesting reactions.

"Do you ever think in Latin, Father?" asked a youngster one day.

"Very seldom, Herbert," was the answer, "but I remember one occasion when I did. I was lying in a Brooklyn hospital of a Sunday morning and I heard a doctor say to my nurse, 'I wouldn't give a nickel for his chances.' And, curiously enough, it was Latin that came to me. I began repeating to myself, *'Deus providebit, Deus providebit.'* "

When the College opened in 1929, the Rector, Father Powers, told him: "We'd like you to carry a heavier load this year, Father Jerry. Besides giving you more classes, we are naming you to the post of procurator."

"Delighted, Father George," Father Jerry answered promptly, and thus assumed responsibility for all the material needs of the College. In addition to that work, he received the job of supervising the erection of an addition to the College building, and those who dealt with him about it were impressed by his fine business judgment, despite his inexperience along such lines.

To the procurator fell also the task of leading the boys in manual labor, and that he found very enjoyable. "Boys," he told them as, clad in his favorite overalls, he met them at the start of the year, "we have some choice projects ahead. Let's take care of them together." He knelt with them in attentive prayer for a moment; then, led by his long rolling whoop, "Let's go-o-o-o!" the company set out, his own zest setting the pace.

The various projects caught the fancy and enthusiasm of the boys. They built tennis courts together; they undertook to deepen the old swimming hole; they repaired various buildings on the grounds. Father Jerry himself drove the ancient Ford tractor that had shaken loose many a mightier man's bones. He held the scoop firmly, even when mud from the spinning tractor cleats covered him from head to foot. His smile shone through the mud, just as his geniality and heartiness shone through all difficulties. The boys loved him and returned his efforts by their hearty cooperation and deep affection.

Each faculty member shared in the prefect work. One evening after night prayers Father Jerry came upon a group of students proceeding to haze a "too fresh" boy who, they decided, needed to be taken down a peg. The unfortunate victim was squealing with discomfort and chagrin as the group held him under an ice-cold shower. "If I were a student now," chuckled Father Jerry to himself, "I'd probably be the ring leader in that crowd." But discipline is discipline, and sparing the rod would be bad business here, he decided. Sternly he called the culprits from the shower room, and with the aid of a handy belt he administered justice.

But he understood pranks because prankishness remained always in his blood. Even in the days when it was his duty to awaken the boys in the morning—a dreary hour for any impulse to joke—he managed to joke about it.

"Father Tom," he said one day to Father Malone, a confrere on the faculty, "I am off to Scranton and shall not be able to get back tonight. Will you take care of the call for rising, please?"

"I'll be glad to, Father Jerry."

As it happened, he succeeded in getting back that night and decided to attend to his duty despite his request to Father Malone. He was up betimes and, as he reached the dormitory to call the boys, he spied Father Malone coming down the corridor. Like a flash, dressed though he was, Father Jerry dropped into a near-by empty bed and pulled the blankets over his head.

"Get up, son," said Father Malone gently as he came to that cot. No movement from under the blankets.

"Wake up, youngster," said Father Malone in louder tones and with a sharp prod. Still no response.

"Here, young man, you get up out of that bed!"

called Father Malone, losing patience and unceremoniously pulling the covers from the refractory sleeper.

"Good morning, Father Tom," said Father Jerry, sitting up with a laugh. "Think of meeting you here!"

At Halloween and on other occasions which called for student parties, no gathering was a success without a song from Father Jerry, and his pleasant voice rang out in "Dwelt a miner, forty-niner, and his daughter Clementine," or "I dreamt I dwelt in marble halls."

There was another—a serious—side to Father Jerry, which was just as attractive. Whenever a boy was confined in the hospital in Scranton, the young priest made it a point to visit the patient every day, though it meant a journey by the slow tram and a walk back to the College. All his efforts brought their reward, for the conduct of his students showed clearly how he influenced them. Many remembered for years how he visited the chapel each afternoon, sitting very straight as he made a meditation, eyes closed, arms folded, his face still and very happy.

"The quality which most impressed me during the two years he was my teacher," wrote one of the boys later, "was Father Donovan's attentiveness at prayer.

At the beginning of manual labor, for instance, he might be as animated as a jumping jack the second before the bell, but like a flash he became serious and prayed very earnestly."

Despite the strenuous activity of these years of teaching and directing, Father Jerry retained his love of reading. When the Maryknoll Superior sent him a book, Father Jerry wrote his appreciation of the kindness:

Dear Father General,
A note of thanks for the *Dream of Gerontius*. I brought it home with me in my bag and read it—and then I read it over again. As with all of Newman's works, I find that each reading brings out new lights and hidden gems.

The spring of 1931 came, and all trace of any ill health or weakness had gone completely. Father Jerry did not know it, but his superiors judged that once again he was ready for marching orders. One morning in May Father Jerry was notified that his name was among the fortunate ones assigned overseas.

"God be praised," he beamed; "this is a happy day. I had resigned myself to the inevitable. I thought I was on the shelf."

The annual assignments were read to the community at dinner but no one was greatly interested at first, for the names were unknown to the boys at the College. But suddenly all were electrified to attention: "To the mission of Fushun in Manchukuo, Father Gerard Donovan, now of Maryknoll College."

There was a breathless gasp—and then thunderous applause. Their own Father Jerry was to go to the field! The student body broke into a frenzy of clapping and cheering.

After dinner as Father Jerry came along the corridor, the enthusiasm still ran high and the boys greeted him with another loud cheer. He signaled for silence. "Thanks, boys. And don't forget—*hodie mihi, cras tibi*—today it is I, tomorrow it will be you. At Maryknoll we all go the whole way."

VI

"Lord, it is good to be here!"

"GO FORTH, ye heralds of God's tender mercy," sang the Maryknoll community.

A century or so ago the French musician Gounod wrote a hymn, delicate, yet resolute and martial, for use at the annual Departure Ceremony of the French foreign-mission seminary on the *Rue du Bac* in Paris. To its strains many Old World apostles of that and other establishments have taken leave of their houses of training and of their dear ones when the time came to begin the journey to Asia or Africa. Now Gounod's hymn is heard on the American continent, when, on the last Sunday of July of each year, Maryknoll holds its Departure Ceremony.

Some thousands of visitors were at Maryknoll on that summer day in 1931. They occupied the quadrangle and the cloister walks to bid farewell to the mission band of which Father Jerry was a member. An altar had been erected in the Oriental kiosk, and

"LORD, IT IS GOOD TO BE HERE!"

behind it hung the hunch-backed bell whose weird notes announced the moment of departure. Once used in a Buddhist temple at Sendai, it had been a gift to Maryknoll from the bishop of that Japanese city. Now it was calling American apostles to bear to the East the message of Christ, and the little company took their place.

The *Itinerarium*, the Church's prayer for those about to begin a long journey, was chanted; then there was an exhortation and a word of Godspeed from Maryknoll's Founder-General, Father James Anthony Walsh. The conferring of the mission crucifixes followed, and the formal assignment of each missioner to his field, "in the name of the Catholic Foreign Mission Society of America and by the authority of the Sacred Congregation of Propaganda." Thus Father Jerry took his place officially in the centuries-long line of apostles authorized to bear Christ witness in fields afar.

"Farewell, brothers, farewell!" Gounod's beautiful hymn filled the summer air. Then came God's blessing in the Blessed Sacrament. There was a last stirring pause, a moment of anguish for fathers and mothers, a moment of mingled pain and delight for the departing priests, a moment of vibrant hope for the men of the ranks still in their years of preparation—

and then waiting cars received the journeyers and swept them down the drive. They were gone!

"The thrill of the send-off was none the less for me because of the three years' delay," wrote Father Jerry a few days later. "It will always be a pleasant memory through my mission years."

Father Jerry had a brief, joyous stop at the College at Clarks Summit, and then he paid his last visit to his home. August 2 was his mother's sixty-ninth birthday and he had the happiness of spending it quietly with her and Katie, even though many relatives and friends claimed a portion of his attention. Mrs. Donovan maintained an air of calm happiness and contentment. Father Jerry marveled at it and toward the end of the day remarked how good it was to see her so.

"Jerry," she said, "years ago when you left me as a youngster, I reminded you that God was in China, too. I repeat that now. He will take as good care of my boy there as here at home."

He gave her one of his long smiles. "You're wonderful, Mother!" he said—words in turn for her to put away in her heart.

One of Father Jerry's calls was at St. Mary's Institute for the Blind in Lansdale, where the children, who already knew him, produced a musical program

"LORD, IT IS GOOD TO BE HERE!"

in his honor. With childish simplicity each announced his or her piece, and Father Jerry had a pleasant comment for each when it was finished.

Little Anna Spaer sang a song called "Dawn." "That was very beautiful, Anna," said Father Jerry; "quite as beautiful as the early morning when a new day breaks." And he added, half to himself, "In the Far East, it is very beautiful when a new day of faith breaks over men's souls."

One girl rendered "Maryland, my Maryland" on the piano, and Father Jerry drew great applause by singing to the tune the Maryknoll hymn. "And now I must be on my way," he said.

"Oh, no!" went up a disappointed cry, and the little sightless figures ran to him, reaching out arms to keep him with them.

"Well, we'll compromise," he answered merrily. "If you'll let me go now, I promise to come back to you as soon as ever I return from China."

"All right, Father," they chorused, "it's a promise. We'll be waiting."

On the third of August Father Jerry left Pittsburgh for the West, and within a few days he had joined his companions on the Pacific Coast.

As the new group was about to sail, a vessel from Japan brought to port a veteran Maryknoller, broken in health after his years in the Orient. Father Jerry discovered that the veteran was without funds after disposing of whatever he possessed in his field of labor. Stealthily in the evening went the outgoing missioner to the older man's room. "Look, Father Jim, I've been given many gifts by my friends, and I can get along without some. I want you to take this." Before puzzled Father Jim could protest, Father Jerry had disappeared, leaving in the other priest's hands a hundred dollars.

The 1931 band was divided on the coast, some sailing from San Francisco, and some from Seattle, which meant a stop at Vancouver. Father Jerry was one of seven to sail with the northern group. On the feast of the Assumption, last Masses were celebrated in America and Our Lady, Star of the Sea, was invoked for a safe voyage. Then the *Empress of Japan* pointed her prow out over the western horizon toward the land of their missionary dreams.

"Goodby, America," waved Father Jerry. "You are something very precious—but something more so lies ahead."

There were bright days and gray ones, days when sea and sky were azure and silver, days when the water was out of sorts and white-flecked waves raced past the ship. There were no great storms, and no great events occurred either aboard or in the world of ocean between the vessel and the horizon.

On the night of August 28 a few faint lights appeared—the coast of Japan. Next morning Father Jerry and his companions came on deck to discover they had entered the harbor of Yokohama. A day was spent in Tokyo, and then it was farewell to the *Empress* as they reached the harbor of Kobe.

"Hello there, Maryknoll!" came a call from the quay, and the group of travelers discovered in the crowd the half-roguish smile of Father Fage, known to all of them as one of Japan's noble ancients among missioners. Every Maryknoll group landing at Kobe had been met by Father Fage, had been saved from much woe by his experience with the Customs, and, too, had been subject to the amiable torment of his banter. But the 1931 group felt that in Father Jerry they had a worthy opponent for his thrusts, and they enjoyed the sparkling repartee of the two until the Knollers waved him goodby.

"Father John, I would a word with you." The group, now reduced to five, was journeying by rail from Kobe along the beautiful Japanese coast to Shimonoseki.

"Yes, Father Jerry, let's hear it," said Father John, his curiosity roused.

"I am wondering if you have sufficient funds to carry the two of us over the rest of the road to Manchukuo—or must I walk?"

"I certainly have, Jerry, and you're welcome to whatever I have." Father Comber had discovered the secret of Father Jerry's gift to the veteran Knoller before they sailed, and now he knew what the older priest had not guessed, that it was not out of abundance that his companion had given, but out of a meager store.

The boat from Shimonoseki to Fusan, the great port of southern Korea, required the better part of a day for the crossing. After a rough voyage across the straits, and a train ride of more than a day almost the entire length of the Korean peninsula, the party alighted at Heijo, principal city of the Maryknoll territory in the northern part of the country.

Here at Heijo the year's contingent for Korea was to remain, and so the travelers were now reduced to two, Father Comber and Father Donovan. "And then there were two," quoted Father Jerry with a laugh. "Looks as if we'll have to do the navigating by ourselves now."

They bade farewell to the "Korean" Maryknollers and proceeded on their way to the border. At night on September 3, they crossed the bridge over the Yalu

"LORD, IT IS GOOD TO BE HERE!"

River and were at last in Manchukuo, the field of their apostolate. A few more hours of train riding brought them to Hun Ho and then to Fushun, where the tedious journey of more than a month came to a close.

"Thanks be to God, there's to be an end of living from a suitcase for a while," said Father Jerry, "though I suppose from now on there'll be plenty of living from a mission kit."

Father McCormack, the Mission Superior in Manchukuo; Father Bridge, Father Jerry's old companion of school days; and Brother Benedict, were at the Fushun station with a heart-warming greeting. An attempt was made to find a taxi but it proved vain, so the newcomers were put aboard a Russian carriage, a droshky—the Manchukuoan substitute for a hansom cab—and the sober horse plodded with them through the city streets.

"I can't find any roses strewn in my path," commented Father Jerry, "but someone has been wonderfully generous with the mud."

"The mission!" announced Father McCormack at last, and they saw before them Maryknoll's compound with its chapel, its asylums, its school, its convent, its rectory.

Father Jerry leaned quietly toward his companion

and pressed his arm. "We are home, Father John," he said.

Travel-weary though they were, the two went to the little chapel to breathe the same prayer of thanksgiving: "Lord, it is good for us to be here."

VII

The New Horizon

NOW came into Father Jerry's life the little red book, the phrase book that was in his hands at all hours. And always there was the language teacher, who endlessly sat opposite him and sang phrases.

"Repeat! Repeat!" he called. And repeating, repeating, Father Jerry obeyed him—blithely at first, he smiling, the teacher smiling. Repeating, repeating —until his smile and the teacher's became fixed, and the teacher's "Repeat! Repeat!" became a trifle metallic and rasping as, with passing days and weeks, what had begun with laughter became unvarnished labor.

"Now I have it," said Father Jerry finally to Father Comber. "I was sure it should be done differently. I was convinced that this was not my way. Perhaps others can learn by phrases, by tuning their ears and loading their brains with sentences, and putting together the language like a jigsaw puzzle. But I can't do it that way. I've worked out my own scheme,

Father John. See here; I've been copying these for three days now. Here I have nouns, adjectives, prepositions. Maybe in this lingo there is not supposed to be grammar as we know it, but I've got to suppose there is. I can remember it only if I write it down in bits and feel that I am putting it together as we would the words in good old *Americanese*."

The older hands at the pioneer station in Fushun smiled and left him to his own devices. In those early days, when there was no language school, each new man shifted for himself to a great extent. But Father Jerry's furious energy and active mind brought all their resourcefulness to the job, and by the rule of trial and error he triumphed over relatively poor tools and began the achievement of what, with the years, was to become a very creditable mastery of the Chinese language.

The language of the Maryknoll Mission in Manchukuo is the Mandarin dialect as spoken in North China, for it is principally from the old provinces of Chili and Shantung that has come the great body of dwellers in this land that lies cupped between China, Russia, and Korea.

Manchukuo stretches to the northeast of China in much the same relative position as the New England States have to the rest of the land of the Stars and

Stripes. There is the difference that Manchukuo is more than six times the size of New England; indeed, larger than New England and all the Atlantic States as far as Florida combined.

Centuries ago real Manchus lived here and possessed a flourishing realm. Mongol invasions desolated the country, but the Manchus remained, though decreasing in numbers. In 1664, by a trick of circumstance, the Manchus conquered China, and they drained their own land of citizens to set up in every Chinese city armed posts to hold their conquests. But the Chinese, quite true to their tradition, proceeded placidly to the peaceful conquest of Manchuria. From the beginning of the nineteenth century, northern Chinese, particularly natives of Shantung, poured by thousands and tens of thousands into this country. When the Manchus were overthrown by the successful attempt in 1912 to set up a Chinese republic, the Manchu people had been practically absorbed by the Chinese. There are today some two hundred thousand Manchus, discoverable only in northern Manchuria, their language spoken only by isolated groups.

When Japan overcame Russia in 1904, she took over Russia's privileges in Manchuria. China sought to stop Japan's progress in this "Balkans of Asia," but

Japan triumphed. In fact, only two weeks after the arrival of Father Jerry and Father Comber, there occurred near Mukden the celebrated "incident" which eventuated in the routing of all troops loyal to China. An independent government known as "Manchukuo" was set up the following March, with the administration in the hands of local officials but with Japan dominating the scene.

When Father Jerry reached Manchuria, the country counted thirty-four million inhabitants who, had they been evenly distributed, would have averaged seventy-nine to each square mile. As might be expected, this was not the arrangement. One very sparsely settled third of the vast area was mountainous: barren and horny near Mongolia, forest-covered near Korea.

Between the mountain regions, the great plains stretched, so consistently fertile that a third of Manchukuo consists of arable land. Though not half of this land was as yet under cultivation, Manchuria was already known as the granary of the Far East. The soya, an oily bean, was king among crops, while "kaoliang," a species of what is called sorghum in the United States, loomed large in importance as food and as a social factor also.

In the ground were coal, iron, and precious metals,

which accounted for the splendid railway system that began at Dairen on the China Sea, connected with the Trans-Siberian line in Russia, and traversed Manchuria east to west, from Korea to the Chinese frontier.

Most of the early Catholics in the land were from the neighborhood of Peking, though there were many immigrants from Shantung too. In 1840 there were only twenty-five hundred, but by 1880 the number had reached ten thousand. When Father Jerry came, he learned that the Catholic body hovered around one hundred and sixty thousand.

During the nineteenth century French missioners represented the foreign forces almost exclusively and it was they who bore the brunt of the tragic Boxer Rebellion. Boxers (Chinese fanatics with a special hatred of foreigners) broke in upon some hundreds of Chinese Catholics gathered with their bishop, one French and one Chinese priest, and two French Sisters, in the Mukden Cathedral, and murdered them all. Fourteen priests and Sisters met death in the region.

During the twentieth century the Holy See intensified its mission efforts in Manchuria, and the area was cut into nine divisions. Maryknoll was assigned a sector in the extreme southeast along the Korean border, a territory of forty thousand square miles with a population of two and a half millions—about the equivalent of that of Kentucky.

Father Donovan and Father Comber had been brought to the central city of the territory, Fushun; a very busy place, they were told, because it possessed the largest open-cut coal mine in the world. Of the nine million tons of coal taken from Manchukuo each year, seven million came from Fushun. Coal, coal, coal—this was the cry in Fushun, and the tremendous investments there had caused the development of a dominantly Japanese atmosphere.

There are three modern cities in the Maryknoll territory: Fushun; Antung to the east, where the railroad crosses into Korea; and Dairen, two hundred and thirty miles to the south on the China Sea. In Dairen with its broad avenues, its beautiful homes, its great factories and busy wharves, one would never dream of Manchukuo as a land of hardships. Outside these few large cities, however, the general atmosphere is reminiscent of western America back in the Roaring Forties. The vast stretches of plains are thinly peopled; sparsely placed, unpicturesque houses mark the scene; the roads are primitive, the vehicles primitive, too. In early autumn one may journey for hours by train and, as far as the vision carries, see only vast fields of deep green sorghum, high as a horseman's head.

That phrase is a fateful one, for when the sorghum is at full growth many a horseman or band of horsemen can travel the countryside unseen, as protected from pursuers as if in a deep forest, and for that reason sorghum has proved one of the major factors in the success of Manchu bandits.

The eastern reaches of Maryknoll in Manchukuo suggest our great American Northwest, with mountains rich in timber and every stream and river bearing logs to the mills. Distances are great; roads, even in tranquil times, uncertain. Communities possess the air of armed camps.

All Manchukuo, save the few cities, is pioneer country. The farmer as he labors with his plow may uncover ancient coins, rare ceramics of lost civilizations, but to him the country is new. The towns, the roads, the local inhabitants, may date back some centuries, but, compared with staid China to the southwest, here are the great open spaces, with the risks of every boisterously new country, with the vigor and opportunities of a land not yet crystalized in tiresome routine.

"Where to, Father John?" Father Jerry often asked during those autumn months.

"I wonder," Father Comber would answer. Together they studied the map of Manchu Maryknoll, asked many questions, weighed every hint and circumstance which might give an indication of the work which lay ahead of them.

On October 9 the first group of Maryknoll Sisters for Manchukuo arrived at Fushun: Sister Eunice, Sister Gloria, Sister Veronica Marie, and Sister de Lellis—a brave band. They took up their home in the simple convent that awaited them and the very next day began to study the language.

The first snow came on October 15. On November 4 the entire mission party trooped across the river to Hopei for the opening of a small building which was to serve as a preparatory seminary, and saw twenty-three young candidates establish their abode there. Father Jerry surveyed this with keen interest, as enthusiastic as the older missioners over this great step forward. With deep interest, too, he gazed off over the wide stream below to the city of coal beyond, not knowing that six years later almost to the day it would be from this very spot that he would be forcibly carried to begin his Calvary.

Four days after the opening of the seminary, the Maryknollers were aghast at some news from a Mukden hospital: Father Davis, one of their company, lay there, ill of a rare disease that had attacked the bones during his years in the mission. Now his right leg had broken while he lay in his bed, and nothing could save the priest's life, said the doctors, but amputation of the limb just below the hip. His career in the mission field was ended.

For Father Jerry this was the first contact with a casualty in action. The frightening thought came to him that it would be a dreadful thing to be cut down at the very beginning of the battle, and he prayed for a long, busy future.

Finally the great day came. "How about a little geography, young fellow?" asked Father McCormack one morning.

"Now, no teasing, please," begged Father Jerry. "Tell me quickly—where is it to be?"

"Hsing Ching."

"With Father Frank Bridge?"

"Yes."

"Three cheers, and praise be to God."

Father McCormack proceeded with the geography lesson and pointed out the way by the map: "Here is a practically straight line, Father Jerry, which extends from Mukden across our territory to the Korean border. It will mark easily in your mind four of the important Maryknoll stations. First stop along the line from Mukden is Fushun, thirty miles from the big city of southern Manchukuo. Ninety miles from Fushun lies Hsing Ching, your station. Eighty miles beyond Hsing Ching is Tung Hua, where Father Comber is to be curate to Father Gilbert. Finally, ninety miles further eastward beyond Tung Hua is Lin Kiang, which holds first prize for remoteness among our Manchu stations."

Father Jerry stared intently as these spots were pointed out to him, and every nerve and fiber of his body, all the powers of his mind and soul, he pledged to the service of his special spot on that map. Already he felt a deep affection for Hsing Ching.

VIII

Life Begins on Muleback

IN THE nipping darkness before a November dawn, Father Jerry hurried into his clothes. The cold did not bother him at all. It was easy to make an earnest meditation and to say Mass fervently. Who could not, when a great world awaited him outside, with the golden pathway of his life work now ready for his first missionary steps?

Through streets that seemed particularly stale and close because they were city streets, Father Jerry hurried to the railroad station and pushed his way into the crowded train with the help of his guide, Father Sylvio Gilbert, pastor of Tung Hua.

The train sped through the city and on through the Manchu countryside, while Father Jerry surveyed the car and his fellow passengers. Here was life in full career: humanity cramming every seat and flooding into the aisle; a babel of shouting in high-pitched voices; enough goods and luggage to fill a market place; blanket rolls stored with purchases and tied with cords; sacks of rice and sorghum; exhausted old men obliviously asleep in their corners; young men and their wives with the spell of the city's sights still on them; babies, bawling lustily, bound to their mothers' sides or backs; groups drinking tea, eating peanuts, passing from one to the other that Chinese institution, the steamed towel; a few men of evident schooling reading newspapers or perhaps a book. Over it all, like a pall, hung the stiflingly hot, unventilated air. It was Father Jerry's first picture of a genuinely Chinese train.

What was all the chatter about, he wondered. No doubt, about shabby little domestic cares, illness, money, neighbors—things worthy enough in themselves but often so unworthily exaggerated, he thought. That sleek old merchant, kindly but smug, rolling himself up in his genteel security, in his easy routine, in his empty little conventions. "This is your life," Father Jerry wanted to tell him, "with some dim, unindulged notion of a life beyond. And the lives of all these others are companions to yours. Would that to all of you could be added something everlastingly worth while." And he promised himself he would try to bring it to them.

He looked out of the window and mused. God

willing, he would never raise a rampart against the winds of the strong, the surging tide of opportunity, the stars of vaulting ideals. He would give of himself, everything within himself, *everything*. This was the morning when life really began. This morning he would resolve it, and he would be faithful to his resolve: he would give everything, and he would take back nothing of himself that he gave.

His guide interrupted his dreams. "Here we are, Father Jerry. This is Ying Pan. Off the iron mule we go, and onto the bony one."

Off they got and, thanks to felicitous plans, found a cart awaiting their baggage and mules ready to take them on their backs. A journey of nearly three days in the saddle lay ahead of them. Carefully wrapped in heavy cotton-padded clothes, the two priests mounted the mules and pointed their animals' noses toward the eastern hills.

Father Jerry's first pleasant surprise was to find that his riding experience on Gunpowder at the preparatory school years ago, meager though it was, stood him in good stead now and he was quite at ease on his mule. Indeed, a little too much at ease, for, as he cast his eyes excitedly toward every horizon, his animal put a foot in a mud hole some two or three feet deep. Henceforth the rider gave only one eye to the landscape and with the other carefully studied the path ahead.

The stop at noon was Father Jerry's initial experience in a Chinese inn. "The first move," explained the experienced Father Gilbert, now four years in Manchukuo and so self-qualified to advise a newcomer, "is to lie down and rest."

"Rest!" cried Father Jerry disdainfully. "I don't need any rest."

"Now, mister," said Father Gilbert in a quietly deprecatory voice, "remember you're in training. Do what the professor says."

Rest they did, therefore, for a ten-minute stretch on the *kang*, the inn's heated brick bed. Father Jerry learned then the wonderfully curative properties of this important feature of every Manchu residence. It was not a bed in the American sense, Father Jerry observed, but a raised surface that ran the entire width of the room from side wall to side wall, some five or six feet from the back wall to nearly the middle of the floor. There was a companion construction in the other half of the room, so that nothing remained of what might be called the original level but an aisle between the two *kangs*. The *kangs* themselves were of brick and packed mud, under which flues led hot air from the fire and thus kept the surface at nearly bake-oven heat. After a few minutes of this, Father Jerry found that all stiffness was gone from his bones.

For a short period Father Gilbert and Father Jerry read their breviaries while Chang, the cart driver, prepared dinner. Father Gilbert was proficient with the chopsticks, but Father Jerry, to save time and not to over-tantalize his ravenous hunger, brought forth a spoon from his pack and for this once at least decided to ignore those Chinese conventions he was so bent on acquiring. He had no difficulty with his *chao-tze* (meat balls boiled in flour batter and dipped in soya sauce), or with the *pai-tsai* (a species of white cabbage), or with the beans heavy with grease. Chinese fashion, the tea came without sugar or milk and was drunk from little cups without handles.

The afternoon sun was warm and even hot. The two missioners, resuming their journey, dispensed with their overcoats for a while and even opened their sweaters. Dusk found them approaching another Chinese inn.

Father Jerry found the keenest enjoyment in the busy air of this hostelry as evening descended. Many travelers had left their mules and carts in the courtyard and were preparing for the night. By the failing light of the setting sun, Father Jerry perched precariously on a three-legged sawbuck in the courtyard and sought to finish his breviary, but he had to confess to considerable distraction. First of all, there were the thirty or forty mules freed of harness after a hard day's pull, which insisted on enjoying a roll in the dust. It seemed the part of prudence to pay heed to their flying heels. And then there was the little circle of half-a-dozen idle drivers and hangers-on who formed about him, frankly curious as to what the silent foreigner was reading.

Among the self-invited, though none the less welcome, visitors to the two priests that evening was a young student who spoke English very well. "I am running away from home," he explained unhesitatingly, and the story had a familiar ring. "There is nothing to do here but farm work, and in the city I can improve my education and serve my country much better."

"I am a Christian, too," he told them almost defiantly, and Father Jerry encountered for the first time that delicate way of distinguishing, out there on the frontiers, the difference between Catholic and Protestant.

"Yes," nodded Father Gilbert, "you believe with the Protestants."

"But they are very good people," said the boy.

[64]

"By all means," said Father Gilbert, and fell into Chinese to make clearer his point. "They are very good people, but they are temporarily separated from the Church which Christ founded. Some day they will rejoin the Church so that all Chinese may worship Christ together."

Soldiers of the village dropped in for news of the war that was raging in many parts between the Chinese who were aided by the Japanese and those who opposed the new regime. They asked the opinion of the foreigners about the disturbances, but they were told that politics are the affair of politicians and not of missioners.

Father Jerry slept well that night, his first on a *kang*. With a small hand broom, one of the servants swept the day's litter from the section allotted the two missioners, paying little heed, it seemed, whether the dirt fell on himself, on the foreigners, or on the floor. Then came rented blankets of dubious state, and Father Gilbert cautioned Father Jerry to roll himself in his carefully. "And during the night," he warned him, "if you feel something large crawling in with you, don't be alarmed. It will not be a rat or a snake, but just the innkeeper's cat."

As did all the other guests, Father Jerry put his feet to the wall and found his head resting near the inn's barrel of strong Chinese wine. Neither the gurgling barrel as it was constantly tapped to quench the thirst of hardy cart drivers, nor the heavy wine fumes, nor the warmth of the *kang* kept him from sleep. The fatigue of a day in the saddle made up for lack of springs and mattress, and he awoke the next morning feeling well rested.

"Now we'll have breakfast in bed," said Father Gilbert. And to his surprise Father Jerry found this was quite the thing in a Chinese inn, since it meant taking what one wanted to eat from a small table set where one had slept. Indeed, it was really a matter of eating *on* the bed and not *in* it.

Father Jerry felt that never in his life had he seen a sight so beautiful as the one he beheld when he rode out into the cold clear morning, out toward the rising sun. The pathway ran at first over a towering mountain, then down a broad rolling plain ringed with great peaks, the whole evidently the remains of an enormous extinct volcano. Crossing the Rockies, he had seen the awe-inspiring Sierra Nevadas; at Honolulu he had admired the colorful heads of Hawaii's peaks; but they both lacked for him the charm of these brown, autumnal mountains of Manchukuo.

"You have never seen anything like them, Katie," he wrote his sister, "outside of the movies, anyway.

Of course, perhaps these seemed to me to be particularly beautiful because they are the peaks of what, God willing, is to be my home."

There were miles, too, through pleasant valleys, crossing and recrossing the same winding river. The water was usually only two or three feet deep, and the riders had only to draw up their legs while the mules splashed tranquilly across to the opposite bank.

When the travelers stopped at noon for dinner, the village police chief visited them at the inn. "*Shen Fu*," he said addressing Father Gilbert very solicitously, "the road ahead is dangerous and I feel deeply my responsibility for you, particularly because America is so friendly to China. I must insist on giving you an escort of soldiers."

Father Jerry thought this a most noble gesture and was puzzled to find Father Gilbert arguing long and earnestly to free himself from accepting the favor. The chief gained his point, however, and took his leave triumphantly amid profound bows.

"Why the fuss?" asked Father Jerry.

"Because all of us, and this means you in the future, try our best to avoid ever accepting a soldier escort. In the first place, we can't afford it, for we must pay the soldiers well and feed them well during their entire time of service. Secondly, they delay us, since it is they and not we who fix the program and the slower we go the better they like it. Thirdly, and this is the principal reason, the soldiers and the bandits are deadly enemies and nothing will draw bandit fire more quickly than a small group of soldiers.

"And remember," Father Gilbert went on seriously, "speaking of bandits, that most of them are just country yokels who have taken to stealing in place of plowing their fields. They have a general notion that the missioners mind their own business and do some good, that they seldom have anything worth taking, and so they leave us alone. But in times of tension and special unrest keep out of their way, because they are then apt to be in an ugly mood. Ordinarily you will have no reason to worry about them."

Despite the fine little speech, the soldiers on this occasion were very much with them still. During the afternoon the going was further delayed by a traffic jam in the mountain pass which lay on their route. The travelers were on the down trail and hence the carts coming up had the right of way—and there were many carts. For long periods the two missioners sat by the side of the road and witnessed chaotic confusion while straining mules, urged by whips and shouts and multitudinous other noises, hauled heavily laden vehicles up an almost impossible grade.

LIFE BEGINS ON MULEBACK

Sleep was delayed that night by certain little creatures that hopped about happily in the heat of the *kang* and conspired to spoil slumber until sensibilities were sufficiently toughened to ignore their stinging advances. Father Jerry quickly resolved on this ignoring and was aided by a heavy dose of fatigue after his second day on the road.

In the morning it was raining, and any hopes of getting to Hsing Ching in time for Mass, even a late Mass, were dashed to the ground. The roads were soggy, and the soldiers were still with them. Father Jerry pitied the men of the escort as he observed them trudging afoot in the mud and rain. But Father Gilbert was wasting no sympathy where sympathy was not expected, and he urged the mules forward so fast that soon they left the soldiers far in the rear.

It was just noon, with the *Angelus* sounding from Hsing Ching's tinkling tower bell, when the two rode into the mission and were greeted by Father Quirk, Father Bridge's curate, whom Father Jerry was to relieve. "Very mean of you," said Father Quirk, "not to have sent a messenger ahead. The schoolboys have been primed for days to give you a welcoming tune with their band."

IX

Hsing Ching Wields Its Charm

IT WAS Christmas Eve, and a gleaming full moon shone on the thick layers of snow that ornamented the Hsing Ching chapel. Father Bridge and Father Jerry crossed the yard for Midnight Mass. As they entered the little sacristy they found it crowded with eight slant-eyed altar boys, all ready for the service, six of them in red cassocks, two in black.

"Look at them," said Father Jerry with a smile, "they are every bit as excited as you and I once were. That's the same stage whisper we used when we were altar boys at home years ago."

"It's the same world," replied Father Bridge with a grin. Both of them were feeling very closely knit to all the world that Christmas night: the world of America, where loved ones prayed with them; the world of the Church, which was paying homage in every land to the Babe of Bethlehem.

Despite troubled times, some of the Christians had

walked as much as forty miles for the great feast. The chapel was crowded from altar rail to doors with grown-ups, and all available space in the sanctuary was tightly packed with boys and girls. How fine it was to be a shepherd among these new flocks in the East, thought Father Jerry as he looked them over proudly.

The little world of Hsing Ching's chapel was bathed in perfect peace that night. But, unhappily, all was not as tranquil outside. Word had come during the evening of two hundred bandits moving for an attack on the town next morning, of their plans having been discovered and they themselves surrounded and surprised by a thousand soldiers. Naturally, no mercy was shown them, and on Christmas Day the victorious troops returned to the town with the heads of two hundred luckless men.

From his very arrival at Hsing Ching, Father Jerry's lot seemed to be to move and labor in an atmosphere charged always with a struggle against bandits. Though Manchukuo had always been classic bandit country, the nineteen-thirties were marked with periods of particularly violent activity.

The first Manchu Maryknoller to encounter outlaws had met the polite variety in the outskirts of Fushun itself while riding to the mission in a droshky.

With soft words he had been invited to step down and sit by the road while one well-dressed Chinese kept a large revolver leveled at him and two well-dressed accomplices relieved his bags and his pockets of all that they could find: seventeen dollars in American money, a watch, a jackknife, and miscellaneous equipment. This had happened the June before Father Jerry's arrival; but a much more serious robbery took place at the Antung chapel in October, while Father Jerry was studying at Fushun. In this case the bandits took away the tabernacle, threw the Blessed Sacrament in a field, and trampled It under foot.

Father Jerry had to spend his entire first winter at Hsing Ching laboring relentlessly at the language, but this did not separate him, at least so far as news went, from the bandit world. Father Bridge was boldness personified and, though conditions were extremely bad, he insisted on carrying through his entire program of visitations, some ten journeys, each of from three days to a week. This had required the better part of three months.

In the neighborhood of Hsing Ching during the winter of 1931, there had been very lively bandit activity, but in addition there was the struggle for political control of the country, and so there were always warring soldiers about. There were also members of the Big Knife Society: bands of ignorant, superstitious peasants, many of whom believed themselves protected by spells from being killed or wounded, vigilantes who opposed everyone who they thought was menacing their homes. Father Bridge had encountered all these groups. The litany of his experiences reads like a passage from Saint Paul. Within a period of three months, he was held up by bandits twice, challenged by hostile members of the Big Knife Society once, and on two other occasions had trouble with bands of soldiers.

Father Jerry found himself breathless in admiration of his superior as week after week he returned with the tale of his adventures on the road. "Someone's prayers took care of me this time, Father Jerry," he would begin when he got home, and then he would start on the details.

Yes, prayer protected him, thought Father Jerry, looking at his confrere, but along with prayer this big-framed and big-hearted priest, who was so filled with devotion to his people, had a fearless hardihood. It was with prayer and courage combined that he helped along God's design, that design so like a flame passed on from bearer to bearer. It was the lessons in ardor and dedication he learned during this winter which completed the burgeoning of the apostolic vocation of Father Gerard Donovan. And it was Father Frank Bridge who did the cultivating of Father Jerry's spiritual field.

Since Father Jerry was held close to the mission compound, he became quickly familiar with the rhythm of life which marked this center of the Hsing Ching area. "My new home here is quite a mission," he wrote his family. "The chapel is about the size of the Hays church in the suburbs of Pittsburgh and will hold well over a hundred. Our house is a comfortable, one-story, brick affair, with bedroom and study for Father Bridge, the same for me, and guest room, dining room, and kitchen.

"Then there is a convent for two Chinese Sisters, one of whom is sixty-five, the other seventy. They have been here for twenty-five years and are worthy old veterans. There are also a school, and an old folks' home, and a plot of land which supplies us vegetables which the cook, thanks to Father Bridge, can prepare in the American way. All in all, we have a snug little establishment."

The school for small boys, simple but satisfactory in its working, had captivated him from the start. "As I sit writing," he said in a letter to Maryknoll's Superior General, "the schoolboys are playing cat and mouse, with our catechist, a sixty-four-year-old youngster, acting as referee. I have to drop my pen for a while and join in the fun."

The inmates of the old folks' home attracted him, too. On the men's side were jolly old fellows, happy to have such a good corner in which to end their days. But occasionally victims of unfortunate circumstances became wards of the mission. There was, for instance, Paul Chi Tsan I, of a Hsing Ching family that once possessed great wealth but that had lost everything when Paul and others of the family took to opium smoking.

Wang, prefect amongst the oldsters, was a character. Six feet tall, with a tremendous beard which gave him a decidedly menacing look, he walked about holding himself pompously erect, a misplaced nobleman who should be strutting in a palace of kings. But, just when his eighty years made him seem unbendingly dignified, he would take to coltish kicking and throw his foot higher than his head.

Lao Li had once been an actor. He gave marvelous demonstrations of changes of voice and could recite classic pieces by the hour. Father Jerry took especial pleasure in watching the placid demeanor and moon eyes of one kindly old fellow, formerly official executioner of Tung Hua.

The home enjoyed great prestige in Hsing Ching, for there, as everywhere among the Chinese, there was deep appreciation of all that was done for the aged. Shortly after Father Jerry's arrival, the mandarin paid the mission a visit and left an offering for the home as a token of his esteem. Merchants in town often donated rice or sorghum, and a number of shops gave wine treats for the great feasts: the New Year, the Spring Festival, and the Autumn Festival.

Father Jerry found that Hsing Ching's Catholics, though few, were held in general respect. Shortly after his arrival, the director of one of the local banks stormed irately because, at the end of a business day, there was an unaccountable shortage of funds in the till. At the height of the scolding, a messenger announced that Chang of the Catholic mission wished to see him.

"What does he want?" he asked gruffly.

"He says it is urgent and of importance to you, sir."

"Bring him in."

Chang, major-domo at the mission and a busy man, entered with calm dignity. "This morning I drew money from the bank," he explained quietly, "and on reaching home I found I had been given too much. I am returning the sum which belongs to you, sir."

Such incidents gave great prestige to those in the city who called themselves Catholics.

Shortly after his arrival the Chinese nuns bought fur and corduroy for Father Jerry and made him the warm but bulging coat, hat, trousers, and gloves worn in that locality. "I feel like a polar explorer," he told Father Bridge as he surveyed his stout proportions in the new garments. But, as the "small cold" gave way to the "great cold" and the thermometer dropped to thirty-five and forty degrees below zero, these articles proved none too heavy for journeys in the out-of-doors.

Father Jerry took great interest in watching the weather as listed in the Hsing Ching almanac. At first he poked fun at what to him was quackish cocksureness in its prophecies of exact days for climatic changes; but time and time again he glanced at its prognostications and found himself saying, "Bless me, if it isn't right again!"

He found delight in the Hsing Ching cataloguing in the almanac. "It's like poetry, Father Frank," he said admiringly, reading it aloud:

January 6—Small cold
January 22—Great cold
February 20—Rain water
March 5—Waking of insects

April 5—Pure brightness
April 20—Corn rain
May 21—Grain full
June 6—Grain in the ear
July 7—Small heat
August 23—Stopping of heat
September 8—White dew
October 8—Cold dew
October 23—Frost's descent
November 18—Small snow

At the first hint of spring, an old fellow whom Father Jerry had not particularly noticed before began leaning over the garden wall, a light on his face like that of a sailor watching the sea. As soon as the ground was workable he started on it, and before long, through his loving care, great masses of flowers began to bloom, set in green shrubbery and clusters of trees. There were big red peonies for the altar, and many of the blossoms lasted until September.

Grape vines, planted by the French Fathers who had been the predecessors here of the Maryknollers, grew near the porch. Many table vegetables came from the truck garden in the rear of the house. Father Jerry made a proud contribution by securing some strawberry plants that prospered nicely in their new home.

By this time Father Jerry was finding the Hsing

Ching charge a very livable one. Sometimes at a day's end in early summer, when the birds filled the trees and sang their vespers and compline and the air was mild and sweet, he was caught quite completely by its charm. True, he would decide, the good missioner never lets his surroundings enter into the problem of doing his work, but, if the Lord puts a touch of enchantment into the *milieu*, there is nothing wrong in enjoying it.

Despite the trying times Father Bridge found it possible to win converts, and at Easter there was a class which brought the year's adult baptisms to forty. Father Jerry as yet did only auxiliary work in the preparation of these converts, but he had a feeling of part proprietorship in all of them.

There was the Han family that eked out a precarious living from a meager patch of mountain land. Father Bridge had attended two of the Han children before their death, and later the father, mother, and two remaining children became Catholics. Another, Lao Hsun, a pagan, did not wish to be separated from his two Catholic children after his wife died, so Father Bridge gave him advice and help, and soon he spoke spontaneously of entering the Lord of Heaven religion. A prim little lady, Miss Du, engaged to marry a Catholic, had quite sagely decided, with no coaxing from him, that she would look into the beliefs of her future husband, and so she, too, was in the feast-day company.

That abstraction, "converts," of which he had so often thought during seminary years, had now become a living reality for Father Jerry. At Easter he stood beside Father Bridge and poured the waters of salvation on those entering the Faith and experienced the true joy of the occasion.

Work on the language was showing results now, and Father Jerry prepared five-minute sermons for Sundays, to which benignly disposed and admiring worshipers listened with evident approbation. "My sermons probably do me more good than they do the congregation," he said to Father Bridge, "but I must make a start. Perhaps the Curé of Ars method of simple, homely instructions will be to the people's liking."

"You do very well, Father Jerry," Father Bridge assured him encouragingly. "Pretty soon we'll have you on the road, a full-fledged missioner."

"Pretty soon" Father Bridge had said, and undoubtedly behind his words was an urgent anxiety to see Father Jerry sufficiently prepared to carry on the work of Hsing Ching as soon as possible. For the older priest knew that with himself all was far from well. Since early May his left eye had been practically blind and now his right eye was affected, and early in June he had suffered two severe hemorrhages which left him semi-conscious for some days.

Fortunately for the ailing missioner, Doctor Leggate of the Scottish Protestant Hospital was in Hsing Ching and he gave Father Bridge a brother's care plus able scientific assistance. He had him moved to a hospital room and in less than two weeks made him strong enough to be carried back to the mission.

But Father Bridge knew he was suffering from a grave disorder, the result of an injury contracted in the World War. Despite the dangerous days, it was resolved to get the priest through to the railroad. There had been no travel for months, but Doctor Leggate generously offered to accompany the sick man, and he arranged for a heavy escort of soldiers. In mid-July Father Bridge was laid in a two-wheeled springless cart, the only vehicle available, and Doctor Leggate sat beside him, while Father Jerry accompanied them to the edge of the town.

"Goodby, Father Frank," he called smilingly as the little group left him. "We'll be waiting for you. Fix up that carcass and hurry back soon."

"Goodby, Jerry." Father Bridge's eyes glistened. "Take care of everything while I'm gone."

Father Jerry watched the cart roll out into the hills, and somehow he knew that Hsing Ching was losing Father Frank forever. His apprehensions were to prove correct for, after attempts to care for the sick priest at Fushun and Mukden were unavailing, he was taken over the Pacific to St. Mary's Hospital in San Francisco, and there he breathed his last in April, two years later.

"Bring me my mission kit," Father Bridge used to say to the nurse, during his last months at St. Mary's, "and put it there on the chair. Let me just dream of those days on the road." And sometimes he would be worried about his young assistant back in Hsing Ching. "I wonder how things are with Father Jerry. You know, the Christians always come first. A missioner can never put anything ahead of his Christians."

"It is all very well to counsel prudence, Father General," he wrote to his Superior at Maryknoll, "but once we are sent for, it is impossible not to go, regardless of the state of affairs or how our health is. My Christians always came first."

Meanwhile Father Jerry, after but ten months in Manchukuo, had fallen heir to a wide-spreading pioneer station located in a dangerous region, at a time that was full of grave uncertainties.

X

Pastor Under Fire

"THIS, Father Alonso," said Father Jerry, "is the Broadway of Hsing Ching. Of course there are no milling crowds such as you see on that other Broadway. There are plenty of coolies here with loads, but there is plenty of room to splash along in the mud. There are merchants, but very few of them are rich, because Hsing Ching has suffered terribly from the fighting. There are shops aplenty but they have little goods, and none of them has anything beautiful or costly; the bandits and the soldiers have jolly well seen to that."

They turned down a narrow lane. "See that cobbler sitting by the roadside. No overhead. And there's a broom dealer, and that man over there has a few pots left to sell. No one has much. Now what would you say this shop is, Father Alonso?"

The curate hazarded the guess that it was a barber shop.

"Right you are; and if you were a citizen of Hsing Ching with an hour to idle, you'd wander into the barber shop and watch the barber do his shaving, the way that half dozen are doing right now. A barber shop here is lounger's paradise. But there is something different about this shop. You see, a barber doesn't usually have so much space as this one has. This shop is a whole *chien* (twenty by ten feet), and it rents for forty dollars a year. Look at that dignified old gentleman on the other side of the room, with a group around him. Don't you think he looks a bit mysterious? What do you think he is?"

"Well," said the puzzled newcomer, "he looks altogether too respectable to be a quack or a trickster." Trying to keep up his part of this rapid sightseeing, he added, "He must be a teacher of some sort."

"Good for you, Father Alonso! One hundred per cent for you! You've hit the bull's-eye your very first day in Hsing Ching. He is a teacher; in fact, he's a catechist. That shop belongs to us, and we let the barber work there to make it easy for passersby to wander in. In prosperous days of yore the catechist was a Catholic merchant along the street here, but his goods went in the crash. Now he receives one hundred and twenty dollars a year from us and is very happy to labor daily to awaken interest in the

Church. He is a wizard at the doctrine and is accomplishing a great deal of good."

So another tyro was in the process of initiation. It was Father Alonso Escalante, come to be Father Jerry's curate in Hsing Ching. He had been a missioner in Manchukuo a bare month, for he had arrived only in September and it was now still October.

Father Jerry had opened his barber-shop preaching hall, as he called it, only a short while before, and he was very proud of it. The Hsing Ching chapel lay on the outskirts of the city and was not easily accessible. Besides, there was the disinclination of non-Christians to approach the foreign priest directly with their inquiries. So the preaching hall became an instrument for an easy contact, and was proving very successful.

Father Jerry fretted at his inability to get into the rural districts, but he tried to offset that loss in converts by more intense activity at his center. One of numerous little means he had devised was to arrange with his better-placed Christians to hold dinners to which certain chosen prospects could be invited. The missioner was present likewise, with a view to breaking down prejudice and to forming acquaintances which might result in conversions. Another effort Father Jerry made was to cultivate the leaders in this town of twenty thousand. Shortly after Christmas he and his assistant presented their cards one morning to the tall man at the gate of the mandarin's home. They were admitted at once and followed the guard through two long courtyards into the private house of the gentleman who served as mayor of the city. For a quarter hour the three drank tea, smoked cigarettes, and talked Hsing Ching affairs, the civilian head of the community showing himself most cordial to the missioners.

Father Jerry, in handling duties as pastor, was frequently in touch with Monsignor Lane at Fushun. In the spring of 1932, the Maryknoll territory had been formally separated by the Holy See from the Vicariate of Mukden and Monsignor Lane was named Prefect Apostolic. During the summer he returned from Maryknoll headquarters in America, to the field to which in 1929 he had come with the original Maryknoll contingent.

"I have my first marriage case for you," wrote Father Jerry to Monsignor early in August. "One of our Christians, long away from the Church, came back about four months ago. While he was outside, his son, now only fourteen years old, went through the form of a pagan marriage with a pagan girl. She is now studying for Baptism, but, since the boy will not be sixteen for another two years, you must decide according to the Church's special laws for China the time due to elapse before the Catholic marriage can be celebrated. The two are to live apart until they can be properly joined in wedlock."

Marriage cases in Hsing Ching were as complicated by pagan custom as they are in all non-Christian lands. Another case was the problem of the Du girl. As a child she had been espoused to a young man who paid her mother ninety dollars in marriage money and then disappeared. The mother later became a Catholic, and Father Jerry, because the man in the case seemed to have passed completely out of the picture, allowed the daughter also to be baptized. But one fine morning in came mother and daughter, white-faced with fright.

"The man has returned," said the mother. "We have offered to give him back the marriage money, but he will not accept it. He insists that he wants my daughter."

"Perhaps he might be won to the Faith," said Father Jerry, hunting for a solution. "Are you ready to marry him if he becomes a Catholic?"

"No, never," said the girl vehemently. "No, I will never marry him. He is only a disreputable tramp. Besides, there is a Catholic boy who wishes me to marry him, and to him I shall be glad to be given. No, I won't ever marry that man."

"He has threatened her," added the mother tearfully, "and I am afraid he will try to steal her."

"Then let her live for a while in our old folks' home," suggested the priest. "He'll never find her there."

Father Jerry decided this was a matter to be dealt with directly, so he went to see the mandarin and told him the story. Later, when the returned wanderer continued to demand his bride, the mandarin came to the mission.

"Let the fellow bring the matter to court," he advised. "So far as being freed of him is concerned, the law is on the Du girl's side. But I shall have to order her to pay back the marriage money, plus eight years' interest at thirty per cent."

The man asked a judgment of seven hundred dollars against the girl and received a decision of two hundred and eighty-two dollars. Immediately the mother and daughter were at Father Jerry's door, anxious now about paying the money. "Father, the Catholic boy will pay one hundred and sixty dollars in marriage money, and her stepfather will pay forty-six dollars. A friend who is sympathetic has offered us twenty dollars. But a portion is still wanting."

Father Jerry slipped out to his desk and set to work with pencil and paper:

Sum needed by girl		$282
Catholic boy	$160	
Stepfather	46	
Friend	20	
Total on hand		$226
Sum needed		$ 56

He looked at the figures. "Why not?" he asked himself. He went back to the mother and daughter who were anxiously awaiting him. "The *Shen Fu*," he said simply, "will be responsible for the remaining amount."

"Just when we are trying to cut down expenses, I was faced with this awful question," he wrote Monsignor Lane. "I know what a feeble-brained wretch you'll believe me to be for not keeping free of money entanglements. I can only hope that some day I'll learn."

Monsignor Lane had to send an admonition, but with it went fifty-six dollars from Fushun's scanty treasury to repay Father Jerry. In May there was a pretty wedding at the Hsing Ching chapel and the Du girl was given in holy wedlock.

"Today the folks back home," said Father Jerry to his curate, "will read the latest news on war and bandits in China. Too bad we cannot tell them about the Du girl, who through many tribulations succeeded at last in marrying her Catholic boy."

Whether or not America was hearing of war and bandits, Hsing Ching suffered continually from that scourge. A week after the new curate arrived, there was a serious bandit attack on the city, but the marauders were beaten off. During that same month Reverend Mr. Henderson of the local Methodist mission, who had brought messages from Fushun to his own confreres and to Father Jerry, was shot during the return journey between Hsing Ching and the railroad.

There were alarms and attacks throughout the winter. Hundreds of frightened townspeople and farmers from the neighboring countryside sought out the mission, and Father Jerry housed and fed them. They quickly discovered that he not only suffered them to take refuge on the Church's property, but made them feel welcome and took upon himself their woes. He went among them daily, giving his smile to everyone and speaking to each individually, continuous chatter that heartened them because it showed his interest.

"How is the baby's cough, Mrs. Wu? Did you give him the medicine?"

"Any news about your house, Lao? Was it burnt in the raid?"

"Did you find your son, Chang? I'll send a message to the Fathers at Tung Hua; perhaps he has gone to the mission there."

"Give that little girl another bowl of sorghum, Han. She looks very pale and thin. Let's keep her smiling."

During the bandit attacks the curate stood in amazed wonder at his pastor's humorous calm. "It isn't the bullet we hear that kills us," Father Jerry would say to the younger priest. "The one that gets us is the one we don't hear." Once as the two priests crouched behind the mission walls with refugees while a battle went on, Father Jerry shouted above the din to his companion, "This reminds me of the World War story about the colored boy from Pittsburgh—he said he heard the bullet whistle twice, once when it passed him and the second time when he passed it."

In the spring the elders resolved to dig a great moat around the town, eight feet wide and eight feet deep, with the earth thrown up to form a rampart for the soldiers. Since the mission was on the outskirts, the formidable trench ate into a corner of the property.

The most stirring attack on Hsing Ching so far as the mission was concerned was that of a September morning in 1933, when the fighting was from the east and south. The mission property was directly in the line of fire, and bullets crashed through a window, broke some roof tiles, plowed through the chapel door, and landed in the sanctuary itself. Most exciting was a shot which hit the chapel bell and drew from it a protest, loud and strident above the noise of battle.

Among themselves the Manchu missioners made light of the bandit peril, but they recognized its gravity. All were in admiration of Father Jacques of the Cha-Kou station, who had saved his curate and himself by his resourcefulness. The bandits had entered that mission and demanded Father Weis, a newcomer, for they wished to avoid touching Father Jacques, who was known and esteemed by many of their number. The pastor argued along with them, finally convincing them that it was not this weak, sickly young man whom they should take, but he himself, who was very strong.

"Very well," they at last agreed, "come along."

Father Jacques prepared everything, led out his horse, and put his foot in the stirrup. "Of course," he said, turning gravely to his captors, "I feel very sorry for you and your foolishness. Once you take me, great armies will come, and there will not be a cave in your mountains where they will not track you down."

"Wait," said one of the men uneasily, and after another conference the band rode off without any prisoner at all.

It was almost another year before Father Jerry could undertake the visitation of the outstations after the manner of Father Bridge. During this period of relative calm, he made several visits to Huai-Jen, an important center some sixty miles from Hsing Ching. This town had had no resident priest for eighteen years although a French missioner had opened the station over thirty years before. There were some good Catholics there, but there were others of questionable worth, a few of whom were reputedly engaged in such evil occupations as banditry and trade in narcotics.

The heart of the missioner was instinctively drawn towards these men and Father Jerry took different means, some mild, some strong, to deal with them. If he could only remain there, he thought—and resolved to offer himself for the task. "Huai-Jen," he wrote to Monsignor Lane, "gives me a heartache every time I visit it. However, I wish you to know that I should be glad to take it over, loath though I am to leave Hsing Ching."

His last visit to Huai-Jen was in December of 1934, and he felt sorry he could not do more for those refractory people. Despite his troubles there he felt that the year had been a fruitful one, and Christmas seemed especially beautiful and consoling. "I only wish I could find words to describe the scene to you," Father Jerry wrote home. "Our little chapel is a gem by candlelight, even if it does seem a bit crude in the strong light of day. The hushed, expectant Christians, the straw-thatched crib, the snowy linen on the altar, the red-cassocked, slant-eyed altar boys, all these made a perfect setting for the Midnight Mass of my boyhood dreams. I would not trade it all for the most gorgeous cathedral in Christendom."

The number of converts in the Hsing Ching territory was mounting, and the adult baptisms reached almost a hundred that year. A special plum in Father Jerry's Christmas pie was a vocation for the priesthood—the first from Hsing Ching. Father Jerry knew that progress was being made and was happy over it. But his deepening experiences were teaching him to recognize more and more the source whence it all came.

"Why does God shower down His graces in this

way on the missioner's poor efforts?" he wrote to the cloistered community at the Maryknoll Sisters' Motherhouse. "It must be because there are others praying to Him—storming heaven—and whatsoever they ask in Jesus' Name, He has bound Himself to give. Thank God it is so, for otherwise ours would be a hopeless task. Roughing it is easy, but to reach the hearts of these people and bring them to know, love, and serve God—for that we must count on your prayers. There is your life's work."

When March made its bow, Father Jerry remarked to his curate, "Father, I'll be off again to a round of the mission stations."

But before he was quite ready for the journey a telegram arrived: "Can you reach Fushun Saturday packed for Lin Kiang? Geselbracht seriously ill. Lane."

Man proposes, and God disposes. There was something particularly sweet about the air of the road around Hsing Ching as he filled his last engagement that Tuesday and hurried home to spend Wednesday packing and giving last instructions. A small bag in his hand, he bade farewell next morning to the Bethlehem of his mission labors. "Goodby, Father. Goodby, Hsing Ching. God be with us all."

XI

Knight Without Armor

THERE was vibrant excitement in Father Jerry's voice. "Wang, we take to the road bright and early in the morning."

"Very well, Father," answered Wang Yun Chang, and there was a deliberateness about him which implied that the veteran catechist of Lin Kiang knew the full significance of the decision his new pastor had made.

Father Jerry was up betimes, said Mass, and closed his kit. Then he and Wang mounted their mules and the young priest's first long journey into the hinterland was begun.

Less than a month previously, the telegram which assigned Father Jerry to the emergency task of taking over Lin Kiang had arrived at Hsing Ching. He had made the roundabout journey of six hundred and fifty miles through Korea to Lin Kiang, and was now some one hundred and seventy miles as the crow flies from his former field of labor, in a world quite different from that of Hsing Ching.

He had found Father Geselbracht, weakened beyond endurance by eight years of grim battling against ill health and the hardships of pioneering, attempting desperately to hold on. "Thanks for coming," the sick pastor had told him; "stay a few days and then get back to your old stand, because I'm not going to quit."

"Of course you're not," Father Jerry had agreed with sympathetic tact, "but figure it all out sensibly. You take a good rest now, and you'll add twenty years to your usefulness. I'll see that not one of your stations is neglected." He meant that, too, for Father Jerry was in ecstasy at the prospect of covering the immense distances in this most remote and largest territorially of the Maryknoll Manchu missions.

"I have the privilege," he wrote to the Maryknoll Center, and there was pardonable pride in his words, "of trying to fill Father Geselbracht's shoes, or rather, his seven-league boots."

Other priests had made journeys to certain of the outstations in this mission but it was Father Geselbracht who had for years systematically covered the ground. He had become known by Government authorities, settlers, and outlaws throughout the region, and seldom did conditions become so adverse that he had to withdraw from the road.

Father Jerry found himself in a city slightly larger than his first mission. Lin Kiang counted about twenty-five thousand souls as against the twenty thousand of Hsing Ching. Besides, Lin Kiang represented greater commercial activity and possessed such modern conveniences as an electric-light plant. It was also a center for the lumbering industry of the vast forest region of southeastern Manchukuo. Around Lin Kiang there was not the smallest remnant of the Manchu plains, or even any wide valleys where farmer folk could build up a world for themselves. "Hop on a mule and ride for twenty minutes, and you are back two thousand years," remarked Father Jerry when they had left the city behind them and come into primitive country.

"See, Wang," observed Father Jerry as they rode along, "how close one mountain is to the next. You climb up one side, down another, and there on top of you is a brother mountain waiting to say hello."

"Yes, Father, and the farms are very few. Many of our Shantung people have become discouraged here and have returned to their old homes in China. This is lumber country."

Back in the hills, on every creek bank, lay logs

waiting for the spring to float them to Lin Kiang, where they would be bound into gigantic rafts and guided down the Yalu River to Antung.

But there was little time for contemplating the scenery. Hardly an hour had they traveled outside the town, when the traffic became noticeably heavy and all of it was moving in the direction opposite their own.

"Bandits ahead!" called a fear-pressed peasant from his cart, and his wife riding behind him was shaking with terror. But Father Jerry and Wang rode on as if they had not heard.

"Bandits!" called a company of horsemen. The American nodded his thanks for the information, but he and Wang rode on steadily. Father Jerry was recalling the early advice of Father Gilbert, and remembering that Father Geselbracht had carefully explained that a priest would never be disturbed by these marauders.

An hour passed, and after a turn in the road they saw faces peering at them from the woods. At first there were a few—then more and more. "There are hundreds of them," said Wang between his teeth, as he kept his eyes ahead and pretended not to see. Evidently here was an assembly of Robin Hoods, and it promised no good for some unfortunate community.

But no voice was raised in a challenge to the two travelers, and they rode on.

In the tranquil light of an April noonday, Father Jerry and his companion approached the village of Nao-Tzu-Kou. "The new *Shen Fu*," said Wang laconically to an old gentleman sitting on a low stone tablet in front of his house.

"And does he not fear the bandits?" asked the elder, looking in wonderment at the new arrival.

The visitors found that, despite the troubled times, the community was gathering funds for materials to build a little three-room chapel, and planning to do the work themselves. The catechist was an open-faced, earnest young man who had gone to Lin Kiang to study the doctrine under Father Geselbracht and had returned to Nao-Tzu-Kou as teacher, working without salary.

Father Jerry felt his heart beat happily as he moved from house to house and marveled at the devotion that had been enkindled in this mountain village. There were confessions in the evening, a talk, Mass the next morning; and then, "God bless all here," said the missioner as he and Wang rode away.

Ping-Hu-Kou, the next stop, was Wang's home village, and here he saw his wife and his baby daughter, Rosa. There was a fervent little company of some fifty baptized Catholics at Ping-Hu-Kou, and practically all the remainder of the inhabitants were at one or other stage of preparation. "Here," declared Father Jerry to Wang, "I must return soon for a week and give a mission to the entire community."

Sung-Shu-Chen, the next stop, was a pretty village near a lovely little valley with fertile fields, but over it hung a shadow: the inhabitants had succumbed to the temptation of planting the poppy, and the opium pipe was proving a great drawback to any advance. But Father Jerry found a tenuous start in some twenty Catholics who were trying hard to persevere in their faith.

Fushung proved to be a good-sized town with a large and steadily increasing body of Catholics. Soon, decided Father Jerry, that would be too important a mission to be handled by brief visits every few months. A priest would have to live there permanently.

"Here," said Wang to him quietly, "there is a difficulty between the town fathers and a certain small group of men who lately have joined the Church."

"What is the difficulty?"

"The town is erecting a shrine to Confucius and each man has been required to give an allotted number of days' labor. These men have refused, saying that it is participation in pagan worship."

"Let us go to the officials," said Father Jerry.

"Do you," he asked these gentlemen after some conversation, "intend to honor Confucius as a spirit?"

"No, absolutely not," replied one of the group. "The shrine is intended to honor his scholarship and to encourage the people to study. The kingly way of Confucius, Father, is not contrary to any religion. The people are free to embrace any religion. At the same time they must conform to the principles of the kingly way."

Father Jerry went to the mandarin for further information and that worthy received him very cordially. "The people call it a temple," he said, "but the official order is to build a shrine to honor the wisdom of Confucius. No worship is intended."

So, far up in these mountains, Father Jerry had found another instance of this problem of modern China and Manchukuo, a problem on which the Holy See had already, as he knew, given cautious instructions. There must be no participation in temple worship, in temple building: that was the ruling. But if there were merely honor to be paid, the Government must be accorded obedience.

"Tell the men to obey," said Father Jerry to Wang.

"And now you are returning home?" the people asked as Father Jerry was preparing to leave.

"No, Meng-Kiang is next on our list."

There was a movement of horror. "Impossible!" they called out. "How will you avoid the bandits?"

"But there were bandits on the road to Fushung," said Father Jerry.

"That was different," the spokesman answered. "Father Geselbracht was well known along that line. But no priest has ever traveled to Meng-Kiang."

"And that is why a first journey must be made. I am leaving tomorrow. As for you, Wang," and he turned in kindly manner to his catechist, "you are free to come with me or not. Perhaps you might better wait here for my return."

Wang smiled his quiet smile. "If the *Shen Fu* has no fears, neither have I," he said.

After all this preamble Father Jerry and Wang looked for an exciting experience, but in vain. After an entirely uneventful trip, the forest cleared and before them appeared Meng-Kiang, which no missioner had ever visited. When they rode into town, a cry of astonishment and delight went up from the twenty-five or so Catholics, immigrants mostly from other parts of the country. Here was a priest at last!

"We all meet each Sunday, and for prayers each

evening, at the home of Miao Chang Shang," they explained to him. And there was something profoundly moving about this little body of Chinese Catholics lost in the forest wilderness, assembling voluntarily for prayer at each day's end, celebrating a "dry Mass" Sunday after Sunday in the absence of any priest.

Miao Chang Shang proved to be a noble type of Catholic apostle. And another old gentleman, Li Yin Tien, Father Jerry observed to be a distinguished member of the community. He glowed with pride to find such representatives of the Faith here. He arranged that night for the renting of quarters that could serve as a chapel, and also for the training of one of the young Catholics as catechist so that this sturdy little group might draw in others.

"Father," asked Meng-Kiang's mandarin solemnly, "do you realize the danger of traveling without an escort? I shall plan to give you twelve soldiers for your journey back to Fushung."

Father Jerry remembered the delay and the cost of an earlier police escort, and resolved not to be burdened with this one. "And what if we were to meet twenty bandits, Your Excellency? What would the twelve do against twenty? There would be no chance to parley, for the guns would do all the talking. My thanks for your kindness, but my man and I prefer to go alone."

Alone they did go, covering the miles—over a hundred—without incident. Faithful Wang was alert to every danger.

When they reached Ping-Hu-Kou again, it seemed as if, as with Job of old, God meant to show His favor by sending the catechist a heavy trial. Within his home town his wife came hurrying up to him, her face sad and streaked with tears. "Rosa—Rosa is dead," she told him dully.

Wang's face was a mask. "It is God's will," he said.

"And the bandits have come since you were away. Your clothes and all our bedding have been stolen."

"The Lord has wanted it so," Wang told her. "The Lord giveth and the Lord taketh away. Blessed be the name of the Lord."

Father Jerry, who had been watching and listening, once again felt deeply moved. Here in this gaunt, hard land of the forest he had encountered life and faith of a sort that would shed luster on palaces and cathedrals.

Curiously, the one meeting with bandits during this journey came only after leaving Ping-Hu-Kou, on the last lap of the trip back to Lin Kiang.

It was mid-afternoon and a mellow golden light was diffused over the sleeping hillsides and brown mountains. The two riders were passing an inn at a dangerous spot in the road when Father Jerry and Wang both heard a distant call across a crest above them. They glanced at each other knowingly: it was the typical warning of the lookout in the bandits' crow's-nest.

Neither was surprised after that call to see an awkward fellow loping down the road, rifle in hand. They halted their mules and he approached them.

"I am the Catholic priest from Lin Kiang," Father Jerry told him mildly.

"That means nothing to me," growled the man. "You two ride in here," and he pointed to a nearby gulley.

Without a word the two mules were turned into the yawning desolate passage, Father Jerry's in the lead. Inside, armed and mounted with many of his gang about him, was the leader of the band. He had never seen Father Jerry before, but he evidently recognized immediately that he was a missioner.

Slowly this potentate of the rude little Eastern court turned his eyes on the guide. "Stupid," he said quietly but with deep disdain. "We don't stop this man."

"You are free to search me if you wish," offered Father Jerry.

The leader shook his head. "No. Sorry we have troubled you; go your way," he said, and there was a shade of deference in his voice.

"Why these fellows treat us so courteously is a mystery to me," Father Jerry wrote home a few days later. "It certainly makes our work of getting around a whole lot easier. Some day, of course, I may meet a crowd who are not so kindly disposed—but I leave that in God's hands."

XII

Eyes on a Prize

THE general situation in Manchukuo by June, 1935, seemed so critical to Monsignor Lane that he telegraphed a bandit warning to every station: "Strongly urge avoid all unnecessary travel until conditions safer."

Father Jerry did not know what circumstances had prompted the warning, but he called a halt to the journeys which he had been making periodically. "You should have seen how happy my mule was when I showed him your telegram," he wrote to Monsignor Lane.

Father Jerry felt the restraint of being kept off the road, but he cheerfully made the best of the prohibition and meanwhile applied his energies to his Lin Kiang flock. He visited the homes of all his Christians and by personal contact tried to lead them to intensify their spiritual life, especially by the practice of frequent Communion.

Even the pagans began to recognize that here was a strong guarantee of the loyalty of Catholic converts. "Once you begin to receive the little White Wafer regularly," they commented, "the foreign religion has a sure hold on you."

In this mission as in his other, the schoolboys captivated him. When he arranged swings and see-saws for the school playground, he found that the pupils returned home only to eat and sleep. "The boys arrive at what would be in America the ungodly hour of six in the morning," he wrote home, "and they stay until sunset."

Father Jerry's favorite project in Lin Kiang was his beggars' home. He was woefully wanting in funds and could not undertake any great charities. But his heart ached for the misery he encountered at every step, and he resolved to play at least a minor role in relieving it.

"Wang," he explained to his catechist, "we shall open a little home for the poor, but for only the helpless poor. In this land and at such a time it would be like shoveling sand into the ocean to attempt to fill the needs of all who are in want. We shall take those who have no family, no dear ones, and those who are ailing. We can't buy much food, and so all who can must go out and beg. Only when begging is impossible shall we use our few dollars to purchase rice to feed them."

The crude house was erected at the outskirts of Lin Kiang, on a mite of land which was rented for nine dollars a year. As Father Jerry had predicted, food was scarce, but at least the homeless could huddle there warmed by the fire, and that was a blessing, especially during the great cold. Soon the police began sending cases, and merchants of the city assisted Father Jerry by sending grain and medicines.

Conditions in the region quieted sufficiently during the next winter to permit several visits to various villages. During the great cold of January, Father Jerry had a glorious experience—a two weeks' journey by *pali*, a wooden sled drawn over the ice by a mule. Wrapped in his awkward-looking but very warm fur-lined clothes, he found it exhilarating in the extreme to swing along over the broad frozen surface of the Sungari River and turn up minor creeks and inlets for his halts. The temperature was forty below, and even lower, but the dry bracing air caused no suffering; in fact, it gave vitality and joy to living.

When he returned, in mid-February, it was to hear news that stunned him by its gravity. It concerned one of his confreres stationed at Lin Kiang's nextdoor neighbor among the mission stations, Tung Hua, ninety miles away.

On February 5, while the pastor was away, a messenger rushed into the Tung Hua mission with an urgent sick call. Father Clarence Burns was alone there, but he immediately boarded the cart and drove into the country toward the village indicated to him. He and Wu, his catechist, were hardly outside the city limits when bandits waylaid them and took them off. The sick call had been a hoax. Father Burns was a captive somewhere in the mountains.

Father Jerry felt the greatest concern. His first act upon hearing of the capture was to call his Christians together for prayer. Each day thereafter there were devotions in the Lin Kiang chapel, and on March 2 his little flock began a novena for Father Burns' safety. When he went to visit the Korean mission across the river at Kangkei, he spent almost the entire five days speaking of the unfortunate young priest held prisoner among the outlaws. "Think how terrible it must be for his folks at home," Father Jerry kept repeating.

When Father Jerry sought to make himself useful in effecting Father Burns' release, he found the authorities very cordial and cooperative. They telegraphed an alert throughout their area, and, while practising the greatest caution and prudence about it, they sent spies into the mountains. That care was needed was very evident when two of the spies were captured and threatened with death. These men, however, saved themselves by insisting they were hunting through the mountains for their horses which had strayed.

On Holy Thursday Father Jerry got what seemed a promising clue. "I have news for you of Father Burns," one of his Christians whispered to him in a low, excited voice.

"What is it?"

"A friend of mine from San-Tao-Kou saw, some days ago, three men carrying rice and flour and sugar up into the country. Whom could it be for, he asked himself, but the foreigner, who must be held in the vicinity?"

"Better still," the man went on, "another farmer in my neighborhood passed the three men and asked them where they were going with their load. 'To Hsi-Yang-Mao,' they told him—mind you how indiscreet they were—'for the Tung Hua priest who is held there.'"

Father Jerry immediately notified the police. The next day came further confirmation. One of the countrymen who had come up for the feast of Easter came to him in the chapel. "May I speak to you, Father?"

"Of course you may."

"I am from Sung-Shu-Chen," said the man. "I met a woodsman from the mountains, who told me that Father Burns had been brought to his house about the first of March and that he had eaten a meal there. The man's house is very near to Tung-Yang-Mao."

"Is that near Hsi-Yang-Mao?" asked Father Jerry excitedly.

"Very near, Father."

"Was Father Burns walking or riding?"

"Riding, the man told me."

"And how many bandits did he say there were?"

"About two or three hundred."

Father Jerry's hopes were running very high. He went again to the authorities with his news; he telegraphed Monsignor Lane; he looked for quick action.

But such did not eventuate. As the months passed, the heavy advantages were all with the outlaws, who could stay in their mountains, remote and safe, in hiding places of which they alone knew the secret.

Father Burns did not gain his freedom until November of 1936, and then not by any direct intervention of soldiers. The bandit horde which held him felt itself hard pressed and planned to kill him, but instead placed him in the custody of a man who was secretly well disposed toward him and who allowed him and Wu, his faithful catechist, to escape. Like one back from the grave, Father Burns appeared again among his confreres. He was given a brief rest, and then he went back again to his post among the Manchu Knollers.

While the soldiers, both Manchukuoan and Japanese, were limited in their effectiveness against the bandits, they accomplished great things by making life impossible for the outlaws except in their mountain fastnesses. Since bands of hundreds and thousands must carry on depredations on a very large scale, it became less and less profitable for them throughout extensive areas of Manchukuo.

Father Jerry had been well impressed by the high morale in the modern forces organized by the new state, and an incident in 1936 brought home this fact strongly. One afternoon in May a peculiar message came to him: the military authorities at Lin-Tao-Kou wished to know what was the proper burial ceremony for a Christian.

"It is rather difficult to describe it to you," Father Jerry told the young officer who came to ask him. "What have they in mind?"

"A very brave Catholic sergeant has been killed

fighting the bandits," said the officer, "and his superiors wish to bury him with full honors according to the rite of his religion."

"Ask the superiors," said Father Jerry instantly, "if they can await my arrival. If so, I shall feel privileged to go and perform the burial ceremony myself." And soon afterwards he was journeying the sixty miles up the Yalu to Lin-Tao-Kou.

As he crossed the garrison campus, he saw that a temporary pavilion had been erected, surrounded by banners, where, guarded by his men, lay the remains of the Catholic sergeant. It was a perfect setting for a military Mass. Father Jerry prepared an altar, celebrated, and gave absolution. Soldiers and civilians crowded around to watch, curious but respectful and orderly. The local officials, the soldiers, the police, and the school children all escorted the body to its last resting place. Father Jerry blessed the grave, spoke briefly on the Catholic idea of death, and set up a cross in that far outpost.

"I wish you to know," the garrison commander told him gravely, "how proud we are of this young sergeant. With only nine men he faced over sixty bandits and held his ground without flinching until death took him. He was an excellent man, a credit to our forces and to the Catholic Church in life and in death. The provincial authorities at Antung have telegraphed a posthumous promotion for him, and it is not an empty gesture, for it carries increased compensation for his widow."

The widow was among those in attendance, a very worthy lady who informed Father Jerry that she was studying the doctrine and hoped soon to be baptized. "My husband," she explained simply, "had been unable to hear Mass for years because he had to travel with his troops. But every evening when he was at home we had night prayers, and he talked often of how all his family in Shantung loved the religion of Christ."

As Father Jerry went back down the Yalu that May evening, he felt very thoughtful. There was death in Manchukuo, it was true; in fact, death behind every turning in the road. But there was life, too: the blossoming forth of nobility in many sturdy breasts, in men who faced their difficulties fearlessly, generously, with their eyes set on a prize for which they fought earnestly—and that prize was the Life Beyond.

XIII

In Borderlands No Longer

"GOODBY, Lin Kiang! Howdy, Fushun!" wrote Father Donovan to one of his confreres in July, 1937. "After being out here in the woods, I shan't know how to act when I get in a big city again."

That morning Father Jerry had received a letter from Monsignor Lane, telling of Father Geselbracht's recovery and his desire to return to the old post at Lin Kiang. "I hope you won't mind the change too much; besides, I should like to have you here with me at Fushun."

Father Jerry was sorry to leave but he was happy for Father Geselbracht, glad that he could return again to the saddle and to the people and haunts he loved. "You know my attitude," he wrote to Monsignor. "My years on the missions have been happy ones, because I have tried to do what I was told and go where I was told. Lin Kiang has been exceptionally pleasant, especially when I could get around to the outstations, and, though I have chafed a bit at the restrictions against traveling, I do realize their necessity. If you want me near Fushun, you have but to say the word."

Father Geselbracht arrived at Lin Kiang early in August, and Father Jerry planned to take his leave after the feast of the Assumption. But he was delayed by news of a wedding, scheduled for the eighteenth. Shortly after the announcement of his leave-taking, the bridegroom came to see Father Geselbracht.

"Father," he began hesitatingly, "both of us studied the doctrine under Father Donovan. He has been very kind to us and has taught us the beautiful things."

"Yes," said Father Geselbracht, a little puzzled. "And what have you in mind about him?"

"Father, our wedding day is fixed for August 18."

"Oh, yes." Now Father Geselbracht understood. "And you would like to ask him to stay over and perform the marriage?"

"Oh, do you think it possible, Father? We did not dare ask."

So Father Jerry remained, and after the ceremony was chief guest at the wedding feast. August 19, then, saw his departure, after a High Mass at which he preached his farewell sermon. The Chinese are traditionally undemonstrative, but Father Geselbracht observed with great happiness the deep affection which the Lin Kiang people had for his young confrere.

Following the Mass, Father Jerry was somewhat nonplused when a committee of parish elders came to the rectory and asked for him. "Father," said the spokesman, "I am not a man of fine words, but all the Christians desire that I should make known to you that when you leave Lin Kiang you take a portion of our hearts away with you. We wish to be helpful to you, as you have been so helpful to us. We are not men of great means but it has been our pleasure to prepare for you a very little sum, the cost of your fare from Lin Kiang to the city of Fushun."

Father Jerry was actually relieved when the ferry drew away at last from the Lin Kiang bank to the river and moved across toward Chukochin. It would have been very childish, he told himself, to show his feelings, but something tugged painfully within him as so many of those dear people wished him Godspeed. It took some time for the lump to leave his throat.

Chukochin, on the Korean bank of the Yalu, directly opposite Lin Kiang, was cared for by another Maryknoller, Father Patrick Cleary. The two missioners had often visited each other during their years as neighbors, and Father Cleary entertained a great admiration for his buoyant friend from across the river. During the summer he had invited him on the only vacation which Father Jerry had taken while he was in Manchukuo. Together they had gone to the peaceful little Korean town of Wonsan, on the Pacific Ocean side of the Korean peninsula, and, by means of a gift for that purpose which he had secured from his family, Father Cleary had artfully contrived to pay all the expenses.

Now Father Jerry, saying goodby to Father Pat, was reminiscent: "Chukochin was the first to welcome me to this part of the world. I remember the wild ride through the Korean mountains, and that breath-taking moment when we arrived at the pass high above the town and looked out for the first time on the wonderland of Lin Kiang and its mountains, waiting for us across the Yalu. Well, now this chapter closes, Father Pat. Let's see what the Lord has prepared in the next."

The following morning Lin Kiang's erstwhile pastor took the queer little Yalu River boat down the stream. At some seasons of the year the river was shallow, and no vessel with draught or a propeller could navigate it, so a flat-bottomed boat had been constructed with an airplane engine mounted above the deck, by means of which the vessel was literally blown the three hundred and fifty miles from Lin Kiang to Antung.

Monsignor Lane was particularly happy to welcome the newcomer to Fushun. He spoke warmly—enthusiastically—with him on his arrival and made him feel at home. Later, alone in his study, his mind kept going back to Father Jerry. What a change the years had made in the young man, he thought. The alertness and cheerfulness were as marked as ever; but the boisterous boy had grown to mellow manhood, the inexperienced missioner had developed a mature and prudent judgment which gave real value to his views. And with this there went an understanding, a kindly charity, that added stature to his likableness. "He will be very useful here," Monsignor decided with satisfaction.

The morning after he reached Fushun, Father Jerry crossed the river and took possession of St. Patrick's Parish in Hopei. It was Monsignor Lane's plan that Father Jerry should assist in central administration work, but he was also to be pastor of this mission of five hundred Chinese Christians and to have the care, within a radius of ten miles, of the Koreans, who were very numerous in this neighborhood.

"You will find me within three miles of the central house," Father Jerry wrote home, "and so, instead of piloting the most distant station, I am now in the nearest."

He had always taken an interest in the Korean people. At Hsing Ching there had been some nineteen hundred Korean families, and he had engaged a teacher and begun a study of their language. At Lin Kiang he had attempted to continue his interest, and one Christmas, in the absence of Father Cleary, he had heard Korean confessions at Chukochin by means of a question book.

Accompanied by a catechist, he now began a visitation of his Christian families. A little later he rented a small house which he converted into a chapel for the Koreans. A convent of Maryknoll Sisters stood near St. Patrick's Church at Hopei and one of the Sisters was assigned to work among the Koreans. She and a young woman catechist prepared to give instructions at the little chapel, and Father Jerry arranged to celebrate Mass there once a month. On the other Sundays the Koreans were welcomed at St. Patrick's.

Father Jerry settled into the busy life of his new mission. Besides St. Patrick's Church building, there were the rectory, the convent of the Maryknoll Sisters and the Chinese postulant Sisters, the old folks' home, the orphanage, the catéchumenate, the seminary. It seemed, Father Jerry said to himself, a little town in itself. "I find it quite a process," he wrote home, "to discover who's who and what's what around here."

It was in reality no problem for him, at least no great problem, for that which many another good missioner might find discouraging—the difficulty of readjustment to new surroundings—never seemed to offer him trouble. He solved it all by plunging readily into each new task as it was given him. When a seminarian at Maryknoll penned a request for a word of guidance, he wrote very soberly to his young confrere: "The physical hardships over here are not what makes mission life difficult. Truth is, the missioner rarely finds that the life is any harder than the ministry at home. The missioner has only to keep diligent, be fairly healthy in body, and of course thoroughly healthy in soul."

To this he added a practical reflection: "Always bear in mind this one great idea: that the priest must be learned and pious, and that both learning and piety mean earnest effort. It is not necessarily the brilliant man who succeeds out here, any more than anywhere else in the world; it is the man who can *keep at it* in face of every challenge, small and great, which God sends him."

XIV

Descent at Nightfall

THE thin-toned chapel bell rang, and Father Jerry smiled as it sounded.

"I shouldn't be hearing that Benediction bell," he said to himself. "If I had held to my plans, I should now be with Father Quirk and well over the Fushun bridge."

That morning Father Quirk had proposed crossing the river to the prefect's house in the city, and he had agreed. Then a series of little tasks had come up.

"Coming, Father Jerry?" Father Quirk had called.

"Better give me a little more time, Father Tom," Father Jerry replied. "I'm still in a bit of a muddle here."

"How about it now, Father Jerry?" asked Father Quirk an hour later.

Father Jerry shook his head. "Sorry, Father Tom. Maybe you'd better go on alone. I shan't be finished here for another while."

"Very well. I'll be looking for you in the city."

"Yes, Father Tom, I'll see you in the city."

The hours sped by, and it was almost six o'clock. Father Jerry answered the call of the bell and started for the church. He shivered a little in the cold autumn air and was glad he had a sweater on under his cassock. Night came so quickly at this season; it was only the fifth of October but already twilight was deepening.

In the south, across the river Hun, lights twinkled in the offices of the coal company and in the buildings of modern Fushun. To the east, on his own side of the river, the walls of old Fushun carried a last faint trace of the sun's afterglow. In the western sky, up the river, Nature, the magician, was switching off the final incandescence of a mighty color show. To the north lay the mountains, bald save for the hazelnut bushes, and in the gathering dusk they were singularly forbidding. They had nothing to offer but enigmatic silence and the wind's moan.

Father Jerry hurried to the sacristy, hung up his hat, took a surplice, and went to the prie-dieu on the epistle side of the sanctuary. His "rookie" assistant, Father Rottner, fresh from Maryknoll, was to give the benediction.

Into the church were trudging old men, a collection of children, orphans and cripples, of which every mission compound has its share, and a few women of the neighborhood. But the congregation was small, for at this season the sorghum was high, and most able-bodied persons were still at work.

Across the bridge from Fushun hurried Sister Veronica Marie, who had been shopping. "Winter is coming," she murmured to herself. "Its bitter cold and long nights will slow up the mission work." She passed through the side gate to her place with Sister Maria at the back of the church just as the rosary was beginning.

Only one person came in later than she: a stranger, who left a few companions just outside. Meeting Lao Kao, the old handy man puttering about in the yard, the stranger stopped him. "I want to get some medicine in the dispensary."

Lao Kao shook his head. "Not now," he grunted. "Come back tomorrow morning. Come about nine-thirty and see Sister Maria."

But the visitor did not seem to understand. Instead of going out again, he wandered on unhurriedly to the chapel, and Lao Kao shuffled off without even watching to see where he went.

The man entered the sacristy, where a seventeen-year-old boy from the seminary, Francis Liu, was preparing charcoal for the incense. Francis looked up inquiringly, but the intruder, ignoring him, went to the door and stepped out into the sanctuary.

The chant of the beads had entered the second decade. Slowly, as if bewildered, the man, holding a paper in his hand, approached Father Jerry. The congregation saw him and suffered a mild distraction. Sister Veronica Marie saw him, too, and, as she prayed, vaguely wondered for whom he was bringing a message.

Father Jerry decided the fellow must have lost his bearings. Genuflecting, he took the man by the arm and led him, unresisting, back to the sacristy.

As soon as they were out of sight of the congregation, there came a sudden metamorphosis. The seemingly casual wanderer changed his whole manner. Like a flash he drew a revolver and, pointing it at Father Jerry, said in a low tense voice, "Come along with me."

Father Jerry and Francis Liu both sprang toward the intruder. "No, no!" cried Francis, "no!"

"Oh, yes!" the man said viciously, holding his revolver firmly in his hand. "Come or we will destroy all of you. We are very many. You come along, too," he added to Francis who, like Father Jerry, was covered by the gun.

Father Jerry understood. After years of bandit experiences, he realized that this time he himself was cornered and that there would be no cajoling himself to freedom, and no saving the others without submitting himself. At this juncture a companion of the bandit, who had followed at a distance, entered and together they led Father Jerry and the Chinese server toward the gate.

In the yard Lao stood aghast. The first bandit, as he passed, handed him a paper. "Give this to the foreign devils," he said in a low voice, leaving the old man staring as if transfixed.

"Take off that cloth," the second bandit ordered Francis, and made him pull the surplice over his head. It was tossed to the ground, along with the censer and its live coals which the terrified boy was still clutching.

But Father Jerry they did not stop to free, not even though the telltale white would stand out dangerously in the gathering dusk.

Some twenty yards beyond the gate, sheltered from view by the old folks' home, three more bandits waited, and together the five quickly bound the priest and boy with ropes. Then they started up the mountain path, a strange party of seven.

They did not depart without onlookers, for an old

man in the rear of the chapel, hearing the heavy voices above the chanting of the beads, had gone out of the front door and witnessed the scene. Two or three other men followed him and gasped with horror. Finally a catechist investigated—but too late.

He rushed back to Sister Veronica Marie, knowing the need of quick action. "Father has been taken by bandits!" he told her. "They are going up the hill back of the mission—four or five in the group."

Sister Veronica Marie did not even answer him. She flew to the chattering men in the yard. "Go after them! Go after them!" she cried. "Why are you standing here and losing precious time?"

The old man stuttered uncertainly. "They are armed, Sister. They are many. And they are great villains."

All too true, thought Sister, as in dismay she looked about at the children, the old men, and the few women who made up the chapel company. But she knew something must be done—her American blood urged her to quick action. Off she rushed, with little regard for religious decorum, to notify Father Weis at the seminary in a far part of the compound.

But by the time he came hurrying up, he, too, could only gaze helplessly at the band disappearing in the distance, Father Jerry clearly outlined by his white surplice. Before the eyes of the anxious watchers, the hurrying group climbed the treeless hill and were one with the twilight.

The workman Lao Kao had by this time sufficiently recovered from the shock to think of the police. "Bandits! Bandits!" he called to the people who were around him, and hurried for the gate in the direction of the police station. But his old legs were creaking and wobbling beneath him.

"Pai," he called to a younger man. "Pai, they are bandits! You are stronger than I. Hurry to the police. Give them this, Pai," and he thrust the bandits' note into the other man's hand.

Pai dashed away with the note and at the near-by station described in a trembling voice what had occurred. He was still talking when Father Weis rode up on his bicycle and added his excited contribution to the story.

A squad of twenty police set out from Hopei immediately. They separated into two groups and, despite the advancing darkness, planned an intensive search. Only a half hour had passed since the capture, and the outlaws were hardly a mile away, so overtaking them seemed a relatively easy matter.

"We shall notify all surrounding stations at once," said the officer in charge. "They are fools, these fellows, to come so close to the city; probably youngsters who have not learned to value their skins."

Word of the capture reached Monsignor Lane at Fushun forty-five minutes after it had taken place. "The police?" he demanded immediately.

"They are in hot pursuit," he was told.

But soon night fell, descending over everything like a great black cloak. From the bald mountains to the north came only silence and the wind's moan.

A council of war was held by the priests and every possible step was taken to put the machinery of rescue into motion. At eight o'clock Brother Benedict left by train to notify the American consul at Mukden, Mr. Langdon. The consul set out at once with Brother Benedict for the residence of the military commander, and there they learned from his assistant that luckily the commander was at that very moment in Fushun, where he could direct everything with no loss of time. "A network will be spread through the entire territory," the missioners were assured.

Mr. Langdon and Brother Benedict went next to the home of Mr. Davies, the vice consul, where a telephone call was put through to Monsignor Lane for a corroboration of all known details. A telegram was despatched to the American Legation at Peiping.

Through the night, at the convent in Fushun the

Maryknoll Sisters kept vigil before the Blessed Sacrament, and the priests did likewise at the central house of the Fathers.

"No word yet?" was the question on everyone's lips next morning. But there was no word.

"There is nothing to be done, then," Monsignor Lane decided, "but wire the Knoll." And far-away Maryknoll was startled by the communication: "Bandits entered Fushun Hopei parish chapel yesterday at six P.M. took Donovan. Good prospects early release. Lane."

Similar messages went also to Bishop Gaspais, the Acting Delegate of the Holy See at Hsinking, and to all the Maryknoll stations.

Beyond this, Fathers and Sisters could only pray or look out over the cold hills and across the empty plain.

XV

Beginning of the Trail

ONCE over the first hill, the bandits, without slackening their rapid pace or loosing his bonds, tore the surplice from Father Jerry and dropped it by the path. They hurried on for a short distance. Then, evidently at an appointed place, they stopped, and other figures appeared in the darkness. Low cries of exultation arose.

"Success, Swang Shan! Success!" jubilantly called the lieutenant of the raiding party to his chief. "We have one of the foreigners. We have an American—a rich American!"

"Good!" said the chief from the shadows. "Well done!"

"We have one of the Americans!" the men repeated among themselves. But all knew they dared waste no time, and the party moved on. With speed but with caution each took up his assignment: both vanguard and rear were to be covered, and certain extra men were to be ready for quick sorties to right or left as occasion might require.

When all was working smoothly, the chief gave his attention to this foreigner who had fallen into their hands. Father Jerry's identity was completely unknown to them and unimportant, too, for he was valued by them as would be a bale of precious silks or a sack of gems. He was a rich prize which would bring a handsome return, they all felt; thousands of dollars, they hoped.

"Well, brother," said Swang Shan to Father Jerry with arrogant familiarity, trying in traditional bandit style to awaken that fear which was to bring maximum cooperation, "it is going to be fifty thousand dollars for us, or we choke you and pitch your bones in a cave."

"*Sui-pien*," answered Father Jerry with a casual shrug, "have it as you will. But you are wasting your time. My Church has no money for such purposes. It is useless to expect it."

The chief smiled. "Words are cheap and easy to utter the first night out. We shall see what you say and what they say after a while."

On they marched with their prisoners throughout the entire night. So well had the road been chosen that not a soul was encountered along the way. After ten miles of turnings through the hazelnut shrubs they entered a forest, still proceeding with no incident to stop them. The stars grew pale and faded. Light intruded in slow, cautious fashion like a scout penetrating the terrain of the enemy. Then dawn came and the party abandoned their trek. Father Jerry and Francis Liu calculated that they had covered some twenty-five miles.

A sheltered hollow by a brook was their stopping place. Lookouts took up positions on the hills and, at the "All's well" signal, one of the men lit a fire. A *kuo*—a species of iron kettle—was produced, and a generous quantity of sorghum. Father Jerry and Francis noted with misgiving that this was no chance escapade but an enterprise that bore all the earmarks of thoughtful preparation.

Seated on the ground, the two could now examine the number and type of their captors. Most of them were not more than twenty years old, although one was really elderly. Swang Shan, the chief, was very young, a sure-moving, big-boned fellow of whose reputation as a petty marauder they had heard. The group totaled hardly more than a score, and all but three held revolvers.

One of the things Father Jerry had never learned to do in China was to eat sorghum, and now, as they placed before him a crudely cooked mess of it, he could only nibble at it and leave the greater part untouched. When the next mealtime came, Francis ventured to say timidly, "The *Shen Fu* cannot eat sorghum."

"Too bad for him," came the answer. "Then he'll quickly starve. That is his affair."

"But if he doesn't eat we'll have a job on our hands keeping him moving," commented one of the men.

"Right," said the chief. "Buy wheat flour for him," he ordered. "Make *mien ga-da* for him; it will be a good investment." And so it was arranged that Father Jerry should have flour dumplings as soon as the meal could be purchased.

There was a lull in the small talk among the men, and the lieutenant of the previous night's raid called out to his chief, "Swang Shan, the foreign devil has very fine trousers."

"Right," said the chief with instant comprehension of his lieutenant's meaning. "Bring a couple of pairs of those cotton trousers and give them to him. Here, you," to Father Jerry, "give your trousers to the man who brought you to us."

With smiling good grace Father Jerry accepted the inevitable. Giving up his trousers, he put on the miserable native ones which were thrown to him.

"The foreigner has very little to keep out the cold," remarked one of the members of the circle, evidently impressed by this gracious acceptance of injustice, something which awakens admiration alike among crude men and fine. "Here is a jacket he may as well wear." He flung Father Jerry a light topcoat, the sort used by chauffeurs and workmen, and several of the band adjusted it on the priest under the rope bonds, which were at times loosened but were never removed.

"And now for some sleep," called the chief and the party crawled to sheltered spots on the side of the hill where the sun could warm them. They drew dry grass about them to add to their comfort. Francis, who had been freed of his ropes with a stern warning not to try to escape, helped prepare Father Jerry's bed and then lay down beside him.

There was silence soon, and Father Jerry used these first moments of repose to try to think out his problem. But the dry grass rustled and Francis moved over toward him, dropped his head on the priest's shoulder, and shook convulsively with soft but bitter sobs. "*Shen Fu*, this is terrible," he whispered. "Oh, this is terrible!"

"Come, now, that's a queer way for a missioner to be acting," Father Jerry whispered back. "You are supposed to be brave, you know. Besides, you have nothing to be afraid of, because before long they will release you and let you go home. Stop worrying. Dry your tears and go to sleep for a while."

"But, *Shen Fu,* I am afraid they may kill you."

"What a foolish idea," laughed Father Jerry. "Of course they won't. They'll keep me with them for a while until they get tired of waiting for a ransom, and then they'll get disgusted and hustle me off home."

Father Jerry was grateful for this affectionate concern. He had not known this seventeen-year-old well at Hopei, but Francis was to prove a help and a comfort during the hardships they were to endure together.

The golden sunlight bathed the weary captives in its warmth, and they drowsed peacefully. But when evening came the air was chilly, and they were happy enough, despite sore muscles, to be on the move again.

Once more the party traveled miles and miles of pathways and roadways. It was evident that the band was well informed and was fixing its route according to the location of the searchers. After three days Father Jerry's feet were swollen badly, and the men gave him a pair of rubber-soled shoes with cloth tops, which were better than his own.

BEGINNING OF THE TRAIL

These outlaws seemed concerned for their captive, and it was apparent to him that it was not merely their interest in keeping him able to travel. They had a code, these loose-living gentlemen of the road, and Swang Shan held them to it. The language of the men in the presence of the priest was never coarse. They never struck either priest or boy. When they stopped a passer-by and took something from him, they gave practically the equivalent in value of the article they demanded. True, if a bandit wanted a pair of shoes from a wayfarer, he who wore the shoes was not free to refuse; but, together with an old pair not so good as his own, he was given a balance of money to make good his loss.

After eleven nights of journeying, the party reached, on the morning of October 16, a shelter which consisted of a roof but no walls. This was apparently an objective toward which they had been moving, for the men showed great satisfaction when they arrived there.

"Now, the boy must go back," said the chief, "and tell the authorities that we want our money."

Francis grew pale and looked at Father Jerry. But the priest only smiled at him, and Francis saw that the announcement evidently did not surprise him. Indeed, during all these hard days, Francis had seen how Father Jerry had seemed to understand the whole proceeding, had done no pleading whatever, had joked with the men and made light of the cold and fatigue. In one thing only he had been uncompromising, and that was his insistence that there was not the slightest chance to get money for his release.

"Here, foreigner," said Swang Shan to Father Jerry, "is a note I have written which testifies that this boy comes from us and from you. I ask you to sign it."

"No harm in that," said Father Jerry. "I'll be glad to."

Another note had been prepared, repeating the original demand for fifty thousand dollars in Manchukuoan money, and Father Jerry saw that this was addressed to the Prefectural Governor at Ching Yuan.

"Goodby, *Shen Fu*," said Francis.

"Goodby for a while, Francis," said Father Jerry, and his smile shone gaily despite his gauntness and the heavy beard. "Tell Monsignor Lane and the others not to be upset about me. I shall be back with them soon. And be brave, Francis. Remember, some day you are going to be a priest."

"Yes, *Shen Fu*, I am remembering. Goodby, *Shen Fu*"—and the boy turned quickly away, fearful lest Father Jerry should see how he was failing in his promise to be brave. But he looked back once more from a distance, to wave a last farewell. "Goodby, *Shen Fu.*"

And he heard Father Jerry's voice, thin and far away, "Goodby, Francis."

XVI

The Vigil and Its Breaking

IN KEEPING with Oriental tradition, Lao Kao, the workman who had received the bandit message, and Pai, who had hurried with it to the police when Lao Kao's legs proved too wobbly, were both thrown into jail and held for several days. It could hardly be, reasoned the gendarmes, that two men so near to a crime could have no knowledge of how it had occurred. But the story of neither proved of use in the investigation, and both were soon freed. So, too, the many clues that were offered by well-meaning persons were found valueless.

The military authorities threw a cordon around an area thirty miles square and tried their best to trap Swang Shan. The local chief of police, pressed by the missioners and by the central authorities at the behest of the American consul, personally directed the search and gave himself seriously to the task. Mr. Ohtani, a well-known Japanese Catholic of Fushun, represented

THE VIGIL AND ITS BREAKING

Monsignor Lane and received each day from the Japanese strong assurances that no stone was being left unturned.

Monsignor explained that the headquarters of the Catholic Church, in Rome, forbade the paying of a ransom for any missioner, since experience showed that this would lead only to jeopardizing the safety of thousands of other missioners who would thereby prove too great a temptation to the kidnaping gentry; however, the friends of the missioners would gladly give a reward to Government agents or private individuals who might help effect the liberation of missionary captives. This news was circulated throughout the countryside.

A direct military expedition against the band was not practicable, since, if cornered and frightened, the outlaws would not hesitate to kill their victim and then scatter in various directions. The best tactic was to locate the band as nearly as possible, negotiate the release, or effect a successful surprise attack. A first move, therefore, was to spread spies and informers through the area. To this end, as soon as reports began drifting in that the outlaws had been seen to the northeast of Fushun, a number of ex-bandits, including a former bandit chief, were sent by the Government into this region.

WHEN THE SORGHUM WAS HIGH

The Government likewise sought the cooperation of the Catholics throughout the countryside, and, to explain how they could be helpful, Mr. Ohtani and Mr. Chen, Hopei's catechist, were sent to the village of Yuan Pu to arrange for a system of contacts. The two messengers of strategy were given a truckload of soldiers as escort. When the great vehicle roared into the quiet little village of Yuan Pu, the people thought that war was upon them and fled panic-stricken into the hills.

The missioners themselves were the best organizers of the Catholics, especially since they demanded no services of them which would mark them for vengeance. Rather, they united them in prayer, and each station held a triduum to the Sacred Heart, with exposition of the Blessed Sacrament. Simple peasants as well as the educated of the cities stormed heaven with moving earnestness for the missing priest. Far up on the Yalu, at Lin Kiang, Father Jerry's old parishioners were in consternation when they heard the news; some brought Mass stipends to Father Geselbracht, for the intention that God might will Father Donovan's release.

Once again the deep spirit of sacrifice always latent in these people came to the fore. A mother of one of the seminarians visited Hopei and asked about

THE VIGIL AND ITS BREAKING

Francis Liu. "How I wish," she said, and there was envy in her voice, "that my own boy could be there in the hills to help Father."

"This is our task, Father," said a Lin Kiang woman, with a turn of theology rather unexpected in the mountain places of Manchukuo. "It is we sinners who must make the oblation for this priest who has done so much good. Perhaps God will accept our penances and bring him back from harm and give him longer days."

One Sunday in mid-October word reached Fushun that Francis Liu had been sent back with a message. Two of Swang Shan's band had led him two days and two nights through the hills and sorghum fields to the village of Ta-Hu-Tun, near the town of Ching Yuan. There the message was given to the Prefectural Governor, demanding the fifty thousand Manchukuoan dollars, an equivalent of fifteen thousand dollars in American currency.

The following Saturday, after being held for some days by the police to aid them in their search, Francis returned to the missioners and gave the details of Father Jerry's first two weeks of captivity. There was a wave of optimism when he had told his story. "A decent fellow, Swang Shan," was the general opinion. "He will do Father Jerry no harm. We shall have our missioner back with much less ado than was the case with Father Burns."

By October 23 the authorities had reached a decision as to the next move. They asked Monsignor Lane for two letters, one in Chinese and one in English, which were to be identical in wording and which were to contain an appeal to Swang Shan to release the priest for the good he and his companions were doing in Manchukuo and to waive all demands for ransom. It was definitely intended as an appeal to the better side of the bandit's nature, and Monsignor was glad to do as requested.

"It is difficult for us to understand why you have taken him," read one portion of the letter, "since he and our other priests have left their parents, their homes, and their country to come to your country in order to do good, and particularly to help the poor.

"You are asking fifty thousand dollars for the release of a man who has sacrificed his life for you and your people. You ask this money of a religious society which gives all it has to charity to help the poor, the old men and women, the orphans and the sick, to educate boys and girls. I cannot feel that you understand all this and yet would demand money for the release of Father Donovan."

The authorities suggested that, along with this letter

THE VIGIL AND ITS BREAKING

to Swang Shan, supplies be sent to Father Jerry, and the missioners prepared such in generous quantities: woolen underclothing, heavy socks, a sweater, bread, cheese, coffee, milk, chocolate.

Four men made up the party which the Government sent to Swang Shan with this plea. How completely it failed was indicated by the fact that only one of the four was permitted to return. And it was seriously to be doubted if any of the supplies ever reached Father Jerry.

After all, Swang Shan was a bandit chief in Manchukuo and his prisoner was an American. In America was California, and all Manchu bandits knew that in California was Old Gold Mountain where anyone could go and pan gold and live happily ever after! Let them send some of this gold to Swang Shan, reasoned that enterprising marauder. So Father Jerry did not come home.

On October 27 justice finally caught up with Swang Shan's band, but whether it struck at its heart or merely gave it a glancing blow, the Maryknollers were never to know. What they did learn was that soldiers had encountered seven of the band and killed one, and that on this man was found the English version of Monsignor Lane's letter. The question remains still unsettled whether this individual was

Swang himself, as some thought, or whether he was merely an emissary going to some learned friend of the chief for a translation of the letter.

At any rate, from that day forward no further word was received from Swang Shan himself, and nothing but vague fragments of information came through regarding his hostage from America. Less than a week after the brush with the soldiers, the story came that Swang Shan's band no longer held Father Jerry. Instead, he was reported to be in the hands of a larger band of one hundred and fifty, led by a particularly cruel and clever leader. Whether this larger band had overwhelmed the smaller one and taken Father Jerry as part of the booty, or whether the smaller group had voluntarily joined the larger one, or sold Father Jerry to it, remained a mystery.

Winter descended on Manchukuo and with it a pall of silence over the fate of the kidnaped missioner. November passed, and December. January was drawing to an end. Each week, faithful to its orders, the American Consulate at Mukden cabled to Washington its report on what became known as "the Father Donovan case." The messages were eloquent in their brevity: "No further information." "No new developments."

THE VIGIL AND ITS BREAKING

"The case," wrote Monsignor Lane in January, "is more baffling by far than that of Father Burns. We knew something about the latter's location and there was contact of a sort, even though very indirect, and we had more information from the authorities because they knew more about the situation."

One thing only continued uninterruptedly and that was the aid to Father Jerry through prayer. The pastor of Chia Shih Mission, an Austrian Capuchin, appealed to his people to pray, and proposed a triduum of supplication. His generous flock trudged each day to the church from outlying sections miles away, sometimes in a temperature of thirty-five degrees below zero. A well-to-do family in Dairen kept a black fast for an entire day.

Protestant missioners, too, gave touching evidence of their concern. The pastor of the Japanese Anglican Mission in Dairen publicly requested the prayers of his people for the Maryknoller, and the entire body of ministers and their families of the Lutheran Mission in Manchukuo prayed constantly for the missing priest.

Suddenly, late in January, evidence from several sources gave birth to new hope. First, word came to Monsignor Lane of a boy who had been with Father Jerry some weeks before, in mid-December. Secondly, good news came through Father Murphy: he reported that, when he was journeying to Fushun from Shan-Cheng-Tze, the aide of a military official approached him, saluted him with a solemn bow, and indicated that he had a message for him from his chief.

"His Excellency wishes me to inform you," said the aide, "that Father Donovan has been located in the vicinity of Hui-Nan-Ting. He asks you to advise the Fathers at Fushun not to worry, for he will certainly be returned to you very soon."

And thirdly, the head of the military garrison at Fushun brought Monsignor Lane the most encouraging news of all. A bandit of the group which held Father Jerry had deserted and offered, for what motive it was not clear, to help secure the priest's release. A plan had been devised, the military commander explained, which, though dangerous, gave splendid promise of being successful. "This bandit," said the commander, "saw Father Donovan as late as ten days ago and states that he appears to be in excellent health."

So once again the faint glow of optimism became a glowing flame for Father Jerry's worried friends.

And then hope was snuffed out by reality, early on the morning of the feast of Our Lady of Lourdes. The telephone rang in Monsignor Lane's study.

THE VIGIL AND ITS BREAKING

"Monsignor, this is John Davies of the American Consulate in Mukden," came a voice. "The Tung Hua military report that the body of a foreigner has been found on a mountain path near Huai-Jen, and from the description we must conclude that it can be no other than that of Father Donovan. You may expect a further confirmation as soon as I can secure it for you. In view of the strong possibility that it is really Father Donovan's body, please let me offer my heartfelt sympathy to you, Monsignor, and to all the Fathers."

Thus the trail was ended, and at Huai-Jen.

Monsignor Lane remembered Father Jerry's letter regarding this village. "Huai-Jen," he had written, "gives me a heartache every time I visit it. However, I wish you to know that I should be glad to take it over."

Father Jerry had returned to Huai-Jen. There would be no more heartache, no more suffering. There remained only the buoyant heart, safe from all sorrow, adorned with the luster of an unselfishness that had given everything, even life itself.

XVII

Missioner's Family

PITTSBURGH'S Tipton Street, where the Donovans then lived, is very steep. Hence perhaps it was the climb that made Father Conroy and the gentleman with him breathe so heavily as they entered the Donovan home that October morning in 1937. Mrs. Donovan sensed nothing in their manner to make her uneasy. When Father Conroy said they wished to see Katie, the mother merely seated them in the room and went off about her work.

Katie was more intuitive and, as soon as she glanced at the pair, she asked quickly, "What has happened in China?"

"This man is a reporter," said Father Conroy. "He says Father Gerard has been captured by bandits and is being held for ransom."

"Well, let's not talk about it here," said Katie, thinking immediately of her mother; and the three went into the living room. Father Meenan of St.

Stephen's joined them, and in low tense voices the kidnaping was discussed.

When the group left, Katie in the *melée* of her racing thoughts found one concern which stood above the others—her father and mother. How tell them? Distractedly for half an hour she walked from room to room through the house, attempting to decide what to do.

Then a shrill call drifted in from Tipton Street— a newsboy's call: "Pittsburgh priest captured by bandits!"

"No use," she sighed, "I must tell them."

But indeed her fears from the boy on the street were groundless; neighbors saw to that. Neighbors possess something very beautiful, that quality which, when one family among them is in trouble, draws all instinctively to its aid.

"Go right along, son," said a motherly old lady who came down her front steps and approached the youngster with the big voice. "Don't go back to that house on the terrace. And don't shout so loudly, son."

Katie's father was preparing to go out, and she saw that delay would be dangerous. She approached her mother first. "Mother, don't be alarmed, but Father Gerard has been captured by bandits. Everybody's sure he'll be released very soon."

Mrs. Donovan appeared stunned, but made no demonstration. She seemed to wish to speak but could not form the words. However, she showed no excitement—only the calm and the quiet which characterized her always.

It was different with the father. He was deaf and Katie had to raise her voice.

"What did you say?" he asked at first, rather listlessly, for he did not understand. Katie repeated. "Captured by bandits!" he cried and started as though struck. "My heavens, that's terrible!" Excitable, and accustomed to solving all his problems, he demanded a score of details which Katie could not give.

At noon a reassuring telegram arrived from Bishop Walsh of Maryknoll: "Cable received Father Gerard captured by bandits from Fushun chapel but good hopes early release Stop Little fear of any other than successful outcome for such an able and seasoned missioner Stop Be assured of our sympathy prayers efforts."

Many friends and neighbors called during the afternoon, and the newspapers kept the family busy. Hence, Katie found little time to think until late that night after everyone had left. When she was alone in her room a sickening realization came over her.

"I shall never rest," she whispered to herself, "until Gerard is found." (While friends and acquaintances everywhere used the affectionately familiar "Father Jerry," to Katie and her mother a strong preference remained always for the more formal "Gerard.")

Next morning there was no news—at least, no good news; and so it was on many successive days. The first report had arrived in warm and sunny weather, but later chill and rain came. Katie found herself distinctly worried.

Then, late in the evening of October 19, one of the Pittsburgh papers called to say that a short-wave radio amateur in Los Angeles had picked up a report that Father Jerry had been released. "Stand by for a further report at one A.M.," said the newspaper office.

Joy approaching ecstasy reigned in the Donovan home. But Katie, secretly, was distrustful. She had a horror of being disappointed.

No confirmation came, but the family did not seem to notice. They reveled in the good news. Katie, however, felt herself racked with the torture of it all.

Then two days later came a letter from Father Joe at Maryknoll. Jerry was free! Had they heard the report? Katie saw that her brother was but feeding hope to the old parents on the flimsy story from Los Angeles. She said nothing.

The next day the newspapers definitely denied the false rumor of the release. However, the first edition received at the Donovan home made no mention of it, and Katie took the sudden resolve to hide from both father and mother this denial. Why hurt them unnecessarily? she argued to herself.

Henceforth it was a daily struggle against any and every circumstance which might reveal the truth to the parents. Each evening Katie hurriedly examined the paper before letting it fall into their hands. On the few occasions when there were items, she managed to remove the page unnoticed. She never left the house for an hour without some ally to take her place, lest a stray caller upset the illusion. It was heartbreaking to hear the dear old lady, her mother, explain to visitors how happy and thankful she was that her Gerard had been freed.

But then came the time when a letter should have arrived from her boy. Twice a day the mother watched for the mail man. "Go down and see if he has something for us from Gerard," she would say.

Dutifully Katie would descend the stairs and return with some such remark as, "No, not yet, Mother."

"Perhaps he was injured or very sick when they freed him," ruminated Mrs. Donovan. Katie watched her sharply for some sign of fading faith and slowly discovered that what she was trying to do for the mother, the mother in turn was seeking to do for her. Each was attempting to protect the other. Neither revealed her thoughts till the end.

As the weeks passed, the vigil became ever more unbearable to Katie. She awoke each morning and a sickening dread passed over her; yet hiding it within her, she sought to be blithe and cheerful through the day. To prepare meals was an ordeal, and to eat them a greater one. Every footstep and knock on the door caused her alarm. She could not read, and formed the habit of walking long hours aimlessly through the house.

And there was the weather, the deepening winter. It hurt to step out into the cold, and it hurt to come back into the heat. "Gerard is out in this cold," she would say. "Gerard has none of this heat," would come the thought.

There was no help but in prayer, and in this she found comfort. Katie had no earthly enthusiasms and regarded as shallow any artificial, baseless buoyancy of spirit. But she had deep confidence in God.

Curiously, not until the Saturday before the news of Father Jerry's death did hope completely wane. That morning she was in town and met a woman friend on the street. "Any news of Father Jerry, Katie?" asked the friend.

"No, not yet. But I'm sure we'll have something very soon now." This had become her routine response through the months.

"Well, I wish I could feel optimistic with you, Katie. But I wouldn't be too sure if I were you. I had a brother among the missing in the World War. I was certain for months that he was alive and finally found that he had been dead all the while."

Dazedly, Katie sought the support of the near-by store front and leaned heavily against it. What a cruel thrust! Others had spoken discouragingly, but this seemed to shatter her last support. When she returned home, she carefully avoided her mother lest she break down before her and admit that she was plagued with the temptation to despair.

At ten on the morning of February 11, the woman from the tenement below came up, attempting to be nonchalant. "You are wanted downstairs," she said.

Katie immediately surmised. She edged from the room where her mother stood, taking the woman with her. "What is it?"

"There are two reporters down there. They say Father Jerry's body has been found."

All reason for restraint was gone. Katie fairly flew

back to her mother. "There it is, there it is at last!" she cried, "Gerard is dead!"

The mother made no reply, uttered no sound, but fell against the wall. Katie wept hysterically, releasing the pent-up feelings of the dreadful months. Slowly the mother came to her. "It is God's will, Katie," she whispered softly. "I gave him to God, Katie. I am sure He has made good use of him."

XVIII

Trail's End

THE HUM of the airplane motor sounded to Father Quirk like the orchestral dirge before the final denouement of the tragedy. With the assistant consul at Mukden, Raymond Ludden, he was flying from Mukden to Huai-Jen for a final identification of the body found on the Manchukuo mountainside. That it was Father Donovan, no one any longer entertained any doubt, but the routine procedure had to be complied with. To the waiting Maryknollers the matter of greatest concern now was the return of the remains.

The air journey was a brief one. Just after ten o'clock on a Sunday morning, the machine curled down to the Huai-Jen flying field. The authorities were waiting, with unfailing Eastern courtesy, and a group of local officials bowed solemnly to the two men as they alighted. It was a bleak February day with a pale, heatless sun. They mounted the military truck which had been sent for them and, as they rumbled off, Father Quirk felt the great cold grip him like a vice.

At least there would now be no more uncertainty, he reflected, and was startled at the satisfaction the thought gave him. For months there had been that ever-present burden on his mind, that load like lead on his spirit and on that of every other Maryknoller in Manchukuo. At least there was no more uncertainty. Doubt had given way forever, and this, after a long night of waiting, had its recompense. But there remained the tragic fact that with the dawn all hope of a humanly happy outcome had departed.

Yet what a privilege, what a glory, it was for Father Jerry and for all Maryknollers in Manchukuo! Here was a baptism of blood; and already, riding in that cold lorry, Father Quirk felt himself distinguished as the sharer in a rare honor.

The lorry halted, and Father Quirk and Mr. Ludden found themselves before a small house in a private compound, which the authorities had converted into a mortuary chapel. At its entrance floral pieces were massed. When the two men approached, guards came to attention. Inside, in the center of the room, stood a large Chinese coffin, its lid in place. Here, too, were flowers and more guards who came to attention.

"May we have the cover removed?" asked Mr. Ludden quietly.

Soldiers quickly complied. Father Quirk saw that the body had been wrapped carefully in a winding sheet of medicated gauze and that it rested on a bed of soft straw. A large white silk cloth covered the head and upper part of the body.

"May the silk be removed?" he heard Mr. Ludden ask, and he braced himself to face what the coffin held.

He knew in his heart what a privilege, what a glory, it was to die as Father Jerry had died. Some day men would sing praises of it. But before him starkly, cruelly, death appeared, and in the icy air of the room beads of perspiration started from Father Quirk's forehead, while every muscle of his body became tense. He felt himself swaying. "God be merciful," he gasped, and put his hand to his head as if he were numbed by a blow.

He must not show too much feeling, he told himself immediately, and resolutely pulled himself together. He was in the presence here of Orientals, who looked for self-discipline on occasions like this. Then his eyes fell again on the face before him, and all other thoughts fled. Father Jerry, who in life was ever smiling, lay here with no smile. Where there had always been vigor and warmth now was only haggardness—a murky white skin pulled tightly over the bones. He who had belittled all pain while he lived could not hide its traces now, for every feature bore the terrible stamp of it, of the long, hard months of suffering.

But there was on Father Jerry's face the mark of something deeper than physical suffering. To Father Quirk came the thought of Christ on Calvary. Was it wrong to make the comparison, he wondered; was it disrespectful, with this picture before him, to imagine he heard Father Jerry calling in anguish on some Manchu mountainside, "My God, my God, why hast Thou forsaken me?"

No, it was not wrong, he told himself. With Father Jerry's faith, his boundless willingness, his understanding of victory through sacrifice, God evidently had asked of him something more than hardships and pain. He had tried him by weeks and months of seeming desertion. He had called upon him to quaff deprivation to its dregs.

Father Quirk left his musing and helped Mr. Ludden with his official task. On a table by the coffin they saw what remained of Father Jerry's effects: the ragged upper half of a cassock; his Maryknoll cincture; his eyeglasses, with one bow broken; the torn fragments of his white shirt with the cuff links in place. And there were the garments his captors had given him: an old padded coat and a pair of trousers, both worn and verminous.

There were no shoes. Probably they had been taken when he was put to death. Two toes of the left foot had been frozen before death: a piece of cotton was wrapped about them. But both feet were in such a condition that it was hard to understand how they could have been used for walking.

On the table, too, was the piece of rope, the thickness of a clothesline, that had been wound double about the missioner's neck; and there was the piece of green sapling that had served as tourniquet. Over an inch deep in his neck ran the furrow made by the rope; the throat was crushed, and the nape of the neck was marked by a deeper hollow where the knot had pressed.

A broken, twisted body, a few tattered clothes, a rope, and a stick—if mere physical things counted, here was the inventory. The examination completed, Father Quirk dropped to his knees. The two Americans then silently took their leave.

The next duty was a visit to the Huai-Jen military authorities, who were waiting to give an explanation of all that had taken place. Mr. Ludden and Father

TRAIL'S END

Quirk were received with deference by the officers, one of whom reviewed for them, with the aid of a map, the entire case, going over the numerous steps taken by the Japanese to effect the captured priest's release.

"Finally," said the officer, "at six o'clock on the morning of February 10, the Nagashima unit of the Manchukuo Pacification Force arrested a Communist bandit named Fu-sheng, who belonged to what was called the First Anti-Japanese Communist Army of the Northeast. Fu-sheng revealed to them that the dead body of Father Donovan had been abandoned in the neighborhood of Niu-Wei-Tou-Shan. In close cooperation with the Kurosaki unit of the Japanese garrison here at Huai-Jen, the Nagashima unit began an immediate search. By ten o'clock, at a point some two hundred yards from the base of the mountain, they discovered the remains of the murdered missioner."

Mr. Ludden in the name of his Government, and Father Quirk for the Maryknollers, offered their thanks to the authorities. When the missioner expressed a desire to return to Fushun with the body, the officers explained that the road was too dangerous and they were anxious to have the visitors go back by plane. The two were waiting at the air field when a friendly young officer came up to Father Quirk and led him aside. "There, *Shen Fu*," he said, pointing to the distant horizon, "is the mountain, sixteen *li* from the outskirts of the city, at the base of which we found the body."

"Could I not visit the spot?" asked Father Quirk eagerly.

The officer shook his head. "No, *Shen Fu*, it is too dangerous in these troubled times. But the Government is marking the place with a tablet, and some day a visit will be possible."

Father Quirk stared at the barren, forbidding fastness and tried to reconstruct the last hours of Father Jerry. When found, the body was frozen as hard as stone, and so for the medical examiner it had been difficult to determine how long the priest had been dead: he was certain, however, that the end had come some time during the previous January.

Perhaps the immediate reason for his death had been Father Jerry's inability to travel farther. From the experiences of Father Burns during his months among the bandits, Father Quirk realized how difficult it was for the outlaws, hunted on every side, to secure provisions. The practice of the first weeks, when special food was purchased for the captive, had no doubt been long since abandoned, and Father

Jerry had been forced to eat whatever crude and ill-cooked nourishment could be found. Growing fear of the pressing troops and growing irritation at the waning hope of any ransom might have made his guards less and less considerate of the prisoner. There were undoubtedly many days spent in warm hide-outs, as the vermin in his clothing bore witness; but these periods were broken by the alerts, when, day or night, the band was forced to take to the road, their prisoner with them.

Quite possibly Father Jerry had had to submit to the indignity common to local captives, of being led by a rope around his neck, the rope attached to the saddle of one of the riders. Weakened by exposure and lack of nourishment, he had been forced to stumble along as best he could behind the horse. Father Quirk, as he stared at the mountain, could well imagine half-starved Father Jerry dragging his faltering feet over the mountainside—until there came a last and fatal fall. "Why bother any more?" perhaps had been the callous remark of his captors. "He means nothing to us. He is holding us back."

Then the decision was taken, the sapling cut. A bruise over the right temple suggested that someone had mercifully struck the captive a blow with a blunt instrument before the traditional Chinese form of strangling took place. Father Quirk felt a certain small satisfaction in the possibility that Father Jerry had experienced no suffering during his last moments of life. And perhaps, because of the Oriental regard for the dead, which among criminals often outstrips their respect for the living, it could well have been that the lifeless corpse of Father Jerry was carried some distance and placed by a road so that eventually it might be discovered and given proper burial.

And thus that tortured body came to rest. Quiet it lay in the winter waste, hardened by cold, buried in snow, and then uncovered by the shrill wind and the gentle sun.

But it lay in peace, for nature is never hostile. Even the wolves and dogs and small rodents which came upon it meant it no disrespect. If, distracted by hunger, they stopped and gnawed at the prostrate form, as the many tooth marks gave eloquent testimony, this was in no animosity of spirit.

Only man can be truly hostile, can show hatred and cruelty and disdain.

XIX

Salute

AFTER the first numbing shock, all was activity at the Fushun central mission. A missioner was coming home, and everything must be in order. The church, the houses, the grounds had to be cleaned and swept, and accommodations prepared for those who would be overnight guests.

To Pai, the head carpenter, fell the greatest privilege. Of choicest Manila cypress, and as designed by the missioners, he formed the casket. The woodcarvers undertook a labor of love and, working day and night, cut the monogram of Christ, the Maryknoll Chi Rho, on one end, and a crown of thorns at the other. On the lid was superimposed a cross and the inscription:

Gerardus A. Donovan, M.M.   1904-1938   R.I.P.

"May he rest in peace, indeed," said Pai as he surveyed the finished task.

Then it was the women's turn. Under the direction of Sister Gloria, the entire casket was lined with a sheath of cotton and surfaced with soft white silk, shirred like the lining of a tabernacle.

The Christians of the entire area wanted a share in the preparations, and throughout the day they crowded the chapels to pray. Many brought Mass stipends. When one old lady of Hopei brought a Mass offering to Father Quirk and he asked if it were for the soul of Father Donovan, she shook her head. "No," she told him, "he doesn't need our prayers. This is for a Mass for the eternal salvation of those who killed him."

In the little cemetery at Hopei, the priests directed the digging of the grave where Father Jerry was to be buried. The great cold was on and the company of brawny peasants who undertook the task had a difficult time, for the frost had penetrated four feet into the earth. The work was almost finished when a cable came from Maryknoll, instructing that the body be sent home for burial at the Seminary.

Reluctantly the news was broken to the workers. "*Ai-ya*, even the body is to be taken from us," wailed one. "Why bring him home? Do they not know that it will only make his father and mother sad?" And the others murmured agreement with him.

SALUTE

At each of the Manchukuo mission stations, the Christians who for months had been praying for Father Jerry's release had been stunned at the word of his death. In far-off Lin Kiang Father Geselbracht found strength for himself in the necessity of serving as comforter of his people. Sobs filled the church when the news was announced, as both men and women wept unrestrainedly for the priest they had loved. What a lesson this would be, thought Father Geselbracht as he looked at his mourning congregation, for those who view coldly the efforts of Catholic missioners in the Far East, could they but witness the gratitude and affection which these people of Manchukuo express toward this priest who had come from beyond the sea to serve them.

Fellow missioners throughout the Far East hastened to offer sympathy to the stricken band of Maryknollers in Manchukuo. From the Apostolic Delegate at Tokyo, Archbishop Marella, came warm words of sympathy: "So good Father Donovan has added his name to the glorious, blood-red martyrology of the Orient. God rest his soul! We are all sure that his sacrifice means an increase of the Lord's blessings and consolations." Bishop Gaspais, the Apostolic Delegate in Manchukuo, expressed similar sentiments.

Striking, too, was the widespread expression of

sympathy from Protestant missioners, and the revelation of what a wealth of prayer they had offered for this man whom so many of them regarded as a comrade in a common cause. Doctor Leggate of the Scotch Presbyterians, the physician who had served Father Bridge so generously and who had cared for Father Jerry during his illness in Hsing Ching, wrote: "Those who endure suffering even unto death in the service of Our Lord and Master have a special blessing. I shall always be proud that I knew Father Donovan and shall always think of him as one who followed his Master closely. My deep sympathy to all your people who have suffered this great loss."

The following Monday an escort of twenty-five soldiers entered Fushun by motor truck, bearing Father Donovan's body from Huai-Jen to the military barracks, where the army and the city officials were to pay formal tribute. When the coffin arrived at the barracks it was buried in flowers. The mayor of Fushun, the chief of police, a delegation of army officials, and many subordinate employees took positions and in order of seniority came forward and made a profound bow before the body. Then a procession formed and, the major officials ahead of the coffin and the minor officials behind, all walked the wintry Fushun streets to the mission.

SALUTE

Night had descended, and the slow toll of the chapel bell began. "Ring thirty-three times," ordered the priest in charge, "one stroke for each year of his life." Monsignor Lane and the missioners waited at the chapel door and the candles of the acolytes served as tiny flares. The remains were blessed and brought inside. The officials participated in the brief ceremony and then with solemn-faced expressions of sympathy took their leave.

Father Jerry had returned. His remains were now transferred to the Maryknoll coffin and placed before the altar, his biretta and a crossed purple stole resting on the lid. From Monday evening until the funeral on Wednesday morning, through two nights and a day, vigil was kept. Priests, Brothers, Sisters—all paid tribute in prayer. Groups of faithful Christians chanted their native orisons. Each morning Masses began at one and continued until well toward noon.

About the mission compound there was one object of conversation—Father Jerry. Every missioner talked of his experiences with him, of happenings at the outstations or on the road, of remarks and witticisms he had let fall, of advice he had given. And among the Maryknoll Sisters who had gathered at the convent from the Manchu houses and from Korea the topic was the same.

A letter from the Sisters to Father Jerry's brother, Father Joseph Donovan, who was stationed at the Maryknoll Center, described their sentiments. "The thing that strikes us most here," they wrote, "is the deep abiding love each priest has for Father. To them he was more than a fellow worker, he was a brother. It would lift the load from your heart to hear all they say. There is no glorification of any kind—it does not belong in the atmosphere here—but there is a wholehearted desire to do honor to their dear one."

For the Solemn Pontifical Requiem Mass on Wednesday, Bishop Gaspais represented the Holy See, and Bishop Blois of Mukden and priests from other stations represented Maryknoll's fellow workers in the Orient. Mr. John Davies, acting consul at Mukden, represented the American Government and was accompanied by Mr. and Mrs. Ludden. Some twenty representatives of the Japanese and Manchukuo civil, military, and police departments were on hand, while the National Defense Ladies' Society sent a delegation. St. Joseph's Church was all too small for the Christians and non-Christians who sought entrance.

Monsignor Lane preached the eulogy in Chinese and Japanese and chose for his text, "He that loveth his neighbor hath fulfilled the law." Deeply disturbed though he was, he found himself desirous of profiting by the occasion to deliver a message to the many non-Christians who that morning attended a Christian ceremony for the first time.

The journey from the central mission to the cemetery across the river at Hopei was some three miles, and again the authorities revealed their courtesy and regard by the public honor they paid the fallen one. Officials directed the long cortege of automobiles from the church to the bridge; and from there on a full military escort was provided, soldiers standing at attention every hundred feet, their backs to the passing file, keeping the roadway clear of crowds.

Though it was not to be placed in the grave, the casket was brought to the spot first chosen for it, and there the final absolution was given. A fall of snow had covered the earth with the white of Chinese mourning. From the cemetery was visible the very mountain path up which Father Jerry had been led to captivity, and deeply impressive was the rigid figure of a soldier silhouetted against the sky, standing on this path at the spot where it passed over the crest of the hill. Thus Father Jerry was completing his Way of the Cross at the point where he had entered upon it.

"I am the Resurrection and the Life," promised the liturgy. And with that knowledge in them, the missioners, a company hopeful and calm and not dismayed, turned homeward again. "Tomorrow," each was thinking, "I shall go on with this labor for which Father Jerry gave his life."

A little building near the seminary became the "chapelle ardente" for the body before the departure from Manchukuo. Three Sisters guarded tenderly the resting place for nine days, and Sister Veronica Marie touched holy cards to the casket as keepsakes for each of her companions in Manchukuo. The Sisters, too, felt themselves a part of a gallant, unbroken company. "Please tell the Fathers," Sister Peter, the Superior, requested of Monsignor Lane, "that we are anxious to do something for them when they return to their posts, many of which are so dangerous. We are going to offer Compline each night in all our houses here during the coming year in memory of Father Donovan, that God may keep them all safely."

Arrangements were finally completed and Father Jerry left Fushun for the last time. "Do you know," said one of the priests to a companion at Hopei, "I feel lonely at heart this evening for the first time in my mission career? It has only now come home to me that we have lost Father Jerry."

Father Jerry's second priest brother, Father Thomas Donovan, was unable to reach Manchukuo from his

South China mission station in time for his brother's funeral, but he journeyed to Japan to salute the remains when they were placed aboard the liner for the United States. In a narrow cabin on the vessel's afterdeck he kept a moment's rendezvous with all that was earthly of his brother.

It did not seem to him, greatly though he would miss Father Jerry, an occasion for sorrow. His mind went back to the day when, on his way to South China, he had stopped at the Preparatory College at Clarks Summit to say goodby to Father Jerry, then serving his term there as professor. "My, I envy you, Father Tom," the younger priest had said.

How many things had happened since then! Father Jerry had come to the mission field, had lived his brief but full career, and had been judged by God worthy of a violent death in the service of the apostolate. Father Tom smiled to himself as he knelt beside his brother's casket. "My, I envy you, Father Jerry," he whispered.

The great ship strained at her moorings. A delegation of Japanese school girls, en route for Hawaii, massed at the rails and, as the boat breasted the waves, they sang a Japanese version of "Auld Lang Syne."

It was as if the East were saluting in farewell.